Prison Break:
The 9 to 5 Escape Agenda

Taking the Leap from Limitation to Liberation

By Clara I. Rufai
Forward by Dr. Ava Eagle Brown

ISBN-13: 978-1537044538
ISBN-10: 1537044538

Reviews

"*Prison Break has inspired me beyond anything I could ever imagine. Clara has provoked me to dream big, capture my creativity, and find my "shine zone" in my world. As someone who has had many "shine" moments, the book has motivated and encouraged me to salute my successes. It has made me realize there are always new opportunities on the horizon that allow me to supersize and share my skills and talents. Clara is certainly blazing a new trail in the field of life coaching, helping women throughout the world reach their goals and their full potential in life.*"

Sherry L. Granader,

ACE, AFAA, NETA, ACSM, ISSA, ASFA, BBU Sports Nutritionist, Writer, Voice Over Actress, Ghostwriter, Nationally Certified Yoga and Pilates Instructor

---

"*I can't say enough about the content in these pages. I loved the Perspective Posturing exercises so much I begged Clara to make them available for download! Her honesty in sharing her story, and the heart she shows in telling it, make this book a great read for women struggling to believe that success is possible, and that it is possible for them.*

I also loved the interviews she included with other people. Each one of those interviews is filled with valuable insights that will help the reader get a realistic picture of what it takes to make it."

Brandy M. Miller,

Author of How to Write an eBook in 40 Days (or less); Creating a Character Backstory; The Write Time: How to find all the time you need to write a book; The Poverty Diaries: Excerpts from the diaries of someone who's been there; The Secret of the Lantern: A Choose-Your Path Adventure for Catholic Kids; and 7 Steps to Change Your Life & the World

———————————————

———————————————

"PRISON BREAK was an interesting and enjoyable read. I like the fact that the style was not too heavy and there were nuggets and tips along the way. It serves as a wakeup call to all sleeping giants to rise and take their places in the battle of life. It challenges the mediocre to ditch the ordinary and dare to pay the price for the extra-ordinary. It motivates the unsure and faint that there is great worth in them and that the world is waiting for them to shine. It presents a strong case for living life fully and compels you to live outside the ordinary.

This book represents the story of my life. Living a life of purpose is the only way to live for me. It is a journey I have started and I am a recipient of its trials, joys, failures and successes. I would recommend the book not only because it is an interesting read but also because it forces you to rise out of oblivion, tackle challenges that lie before you and be the best you can be.

This is great read for people who are unsure and unaware of the strengths they possess, people dealing with low self-esteem and people trying to decide whether to take a plunge out of a 9-5 or not. It is also relevant for people who are tired of their current situations and need a jolt to make that bold move.

The key take away for me was this: Know who you are and craft a mission statement that guides your life and keeps you on track."

Sola Oguche-Agudah
Productivity and Organizing Expert, Writer, Speaker, Coach & Author, 'Zara: Love and Second Chances'

"This book gives a lot of food for thought for those who are struggling with the 9-5 grind, seemingly with no light at the tunnel. The operative work is 'tunnel' – the 9 to 5 creates a tunnel vision mentality which, sadly, then becomes the norm for many. A highly recommended read."

Lily Mensah Yeboah,

Award-winning coach, Speaker, Personal brand strategist, Branded LinkedIn Makeover analyst

Lyncs Media - www.lyncsmedia.com

"The book is an inspirational road map for anyone navigating their way into purpose. There are many who need this map!

*I applaud Clara's bravery not just for taking the leap but also for sharing the intimate details of her journey. I found this quote most profound in her story – **"no one takes your voice away from you, you lose it because you refuse to use it"**.*

The book in my opinion is more than a map for navigating life outside the 9 to 5. It is more of personal discovery – finding and doing those things that bring the deepest fulfilment. It is about birthing excellence – and excellence happens when we break the mould.

Does this then mean we should all escape structured salaried careers? That's not what I get from this book. I get a sense of individuality – find what it is that matters the most to you and develop your essence therein. In or out the structured 9 to 5, being authentic takes a lot of courage. That's the courage Clara displayed in her journey, bravery in documenting it and audacity in sharing it publicly."

ID Ogufere - Financial & Credit Risk Analyst and a Certified Human Resources Manager. Author of 'Battered Roses'

_____

_____

"I have read many books on motivation, this is not just another one of them. This is a story of a woman in on-going embrace of truths she teaches. The author has done a fantastic job of drawing inspiration from ordinary women and men who bravely advance in the face of obstacles to reach their goals – an army of people who refuse to give up."

Moses Ida-Michaels, IT Consultant, Entrepreneur, Minister, Mentor

_____

_____

Dedication

This Book Is Dedicated To The Evergreen Memories Of:

My beloved Dad: I remember the selfless and loving father you were. I salute your charitable heart and generous spirit. You were a father and provider to many, not just to the children of your loins. Living up to your stellar example of love and charity is a tough call, but I'm trying my best each day to do you proud! It was a privilege to call you Daddy - and I miss you still!

My sweet little sisters, Ibifuro Queenette and Ibinabo Victoria: I remember you as innocent and beautiful teenagers, carefree and happy. Despite the lack of luxury, your joy came from deep down, often bubbling up to the surface, which made me love you so. I take comfort knowing your watery grave is replaced by the beautiful vistas of heaven.

This Book Is Also Dedicated To:

My Comrades-In-Escape: Those who dare to embark on the journey from the 9 to 5 limitation to liberation, from grind to glory, from containment to creativity, from treadmill to triumph, from fear to personal brilliance and from prison to palace. It is for you and of you that I write. While I write of myself, I write for you. I learned so much from writing this book and it is my hope, my belief, that you will learn something from reading it. This book is both a wake-up call to your bold spirit and a salute to your sure success - now GET UP and GO SHINE!

Table of Contents

Foreword

Today, I am a Heart-Centered Coach, trainer, consultant, speaker, and author of several books, including Bamboo and Fern, which was re-written into The Mango Girl, which is currently being made into a Hollywood feature film. Less than 8 months ago, I too was caught in a corporate cubicle. I have worked in banking, retail management, sales, telecoms, and a variety of 9 to 5 jobs. I hated them all.

I felt imprisoned and torn between what was most important to me – paying the bills or being there for my kids who needed me at school recitals, the GP, and school trips. I felt enslaved by bosses who were less educated and less articulate but who ruled, not managed, over my being. In my mind, slavery hadn't been abolished, just reshaped. Growing up in Jamaica, where I was told to say, "No" rather than "I am afraid not," proved a challenge for me in Great Britain.

Maybe I never would have found the courage to take that leap of faith if it wasn't for my daughter's illness. She was scheduled for eye surgery after being blind for some time. My boss gave me a huge hassle about taking time off, even though I was still getting work done from home. That was my final straw. They made it easy for me. I don't know if you have ever seen a mother hen and her chick, but touch one and she becomes a beast. That was me. I was in 'beast mode' from there on.

I had already started planning my prison break: coaching clients late at night, speaking, writing, being coached by others so that I could improve my craft, and working towards the day of freedom. It came sooner than I expected or planned, but I have no regrets about that. Although that made it a fearful and nerve-wracking experience, I absolutely needed that push as I was too scared to make the jump. The lesson here is sometimes you have to jump and grow wings on your way down.

I was on my own, supporting two kids with all the bills and the debt you could imagine, coupled with legal fees from battling my ex-husband in court. As scared as I was on the day that I quit, in hindsight, the transition was easy for me – mainly because of the 'backstage' preparation I was doing. A lesson here: work on your hustle while on the plantation.

Financially, there was a pinch and a struggle, but I felt free - freer than I ever felt in my life! I got the chance to spend quality time with my kids, which frankly, was a priceless treasure. I was no longer missing school plays, GP visits, and I was living on my own terms. The fact that this all happened the year my daughter was transitioning to university made it even more rewarding.

We got to spend that quality time together. I wouldn't trade it for a world of diamonds. Specifically, my ability to form strategic alliances has been the key to my success. This will be invaluable to you as you go along, too.

I would like to thank the gutsy and determined Clara Rufai for including me in her audacious and ambitious project to address the challenges of individuals, especially women, who may be looking to transition out of their 9 to 5 prison. In this book, Clara lays out smart strategies and a roadmap that you will find useful as you plan your *Escape Agenda*.

I would like to add a few nuggets of my own to help you make good your escape:

1. Plan, plan, plan.
2. Invest in your craft. Invest in a coach or mentor to help you. This cannot be stressed enough. When I was starting out, I hired four.
3. Know what you are going to do, test that it is needed, and have a Unique Selling Position.
4. Don't be afraid to jump and grow wings on your way down. Don't act on emotions, but on a stable foundation.
5. Try to have a backup plan always – if this plan doesn't work, what else will you do?
6. Network, network, network.
7. Once you break free of your prison, be unapologetic about your decision. Stop letting what other people say hold you back.

It is not an easy journey to get from life on the inside to freedom on the outside, but trust me, you will love it out here! You will enjoy living life on your own terms, whether it be spending time with your children or spending your time doing those things that matter most to you. If you're like me, a rebel at heart who hates rules, you'll one day look back and realize you wouldn't have it any other way!

It is my belief that what you will find within the pages of this book will help you to analyse your situation, consider where you're at and where you would like to be, and what you'll require to get you from where you are to where you want to be.

Dr. Ava Eagle Brown, Author of *The Mango Girl*- The Hollywood Feature Film, International Speaker, Transformational Coach, Book Coach, Sales Trainer, Consultant and United Nations Peace Awardee.

Facebook: https://www.facebook.com/avaeaglebrown/?fref=ts

Website: http://avaeaglebrown.com

Twitter: @AvaBrown24

This book is for you if:

You are ready to consider exchanging your pre-occupation with your 9 to 5 career for a life of purpose and passion.

You are ready to turn your passion and your talent into an income generating idea that adds value to others.

You are ready to own your entrepreneurial calling and do what resonates and lights your soul on fire.

You are ready to ditch the title and identity others have given you, and be your true, authentic self

You feel confined by your current situation or circumstances and want to release your creative potential.

You feel unfulfilled in your 9 to 5 job and would like more freedom of time, income, impact, and influence.

You are sick of sitting in a corporate cubicle and need courage to boldly pursue other alternatives.

You are tired of working harder yet having less time to do what truly matters to you.

You are stressed out from being pulled in all directions, with everyone wanting a piece of you.

You want to quit running the rat race and would like to start running your own race.

You would like to design your life around freedom, finances, and fulfilment.

You would like to exchange the confusion you feel for clarity about your life.

You are seeking inspiration to advance to the next chapter of your life.

You battle feelings of inadequacy and want more out of life.

You either hate or are not passionate about your 9 to 5.

You are in your 9 to 5 just to put bread on the table.

You are thinking there has to be more to life.

You have a message that needs to come out.

You want to escape from grind to glory.

You would like to try something new.

You are tenacious and resilient.

You are bold and courageous.

You are curious to know more.

You want to invest in you.

You believe you matter.

Introduction

The Caged Bird Sings Of Freedom

The caged bird sings,

with fearful trill,

of the things unknown,

but longed for still,

and his tune is heard,

on the distant hill,

for the caged bird

sings of freedom.

- Maya Angelou

American poet, memoirist, and civil rights activist Maya Angelou is one of many women from whom I draw inspiration. This phenomenal woman first wrote her Caged Bird poem in the year of my birth. Decades later, I am encouraged that like millions of people all over the world, I can still draw inspiration from it. While writing this book, I was reminded repeatedly of the stirring words of her inspirational poem.

The conflicting words 'caged' and 'freedom,' in particular, kept resonating deep within my spirit. In recent years, I've found myself pondering on these words and the perceptions they represent. As I concluded the writing of this book, however, I gained clear insight and illumination; I can now declare with personal understanding: *'I too know why the caged bird sings: it truly sings of freedom.'*

When a person feels caged or restricted, it is a big deal. It is an even bigger deal when a person remains so long in confinement that they resign themselves to that state and it becomes their 'new normal.' They completely buy into the lie that *'there is no way out, this is how it is meant to be.'*

Strangely, however, some of the most creative people who ever lived will tell you, if you ask them, that the place of confinement and restriction is often the very place where they've birthed their best works.

How? It takes a certain character disposition, as well as a knowing, a conviction, and an unrelenting application of certain universal principles.

The purpose of this book is not to tell fanciful fables but to tell you my story, from my perspective, so that in it you might find hope and glean pearls of wisdom from the lessons that I have learned along the way.

In it, I will share strategies, tips, tools, and thought-provoking reflections to engage your mind. I hope these propel you forward as you consider breaking out of containment and journeying toward the next chapter of your life.

This book is written not to entertain, but to challenge your thoughts about what is possible, to trigger objective self-analysis, to encourage you to examine your thought patterns and engage in perspective re-posturing.

If it does only this for you, this book would have achieved its reason for being. If it goes further to provoke you to action and push you to finally embark on the journey from where you are to where you want to be - well, that would be the proverbial cherry on top of the cake.

This book does not claim to have all the answers. It promises neither a magic potion nor a one-size-fits-all solution for overnight success. Rather, it shares one woman's story, told with honesty, and some of her hard-learned secrets to help YOU plan and make good your escape from whatever prison may currently be holding you captive.

As a bonus, it is chock-full of opportunities for reflection and inspiring reminders to rejoice in the fact that there's a palace right up the road from the prison.

PART 1 - The PRISON

(And The Limitations)

Chapter 1:
9 To 5 Prisoner Profile

It is nearly 6 a.m. when I wake up to use the bathroom. I get out of bed and that's the last thing I remember. When I come to, I find I am on the floor. The left side of my face hurts like crazy. I try to touch it and the pain is excruciating. My teeth on the left side of my face all feel sore, as does my left cheekbone.

It starts to swell and does not look pretty at all. I try to move and my whole body hurts. I lay back down gingerly and try to remember what happened. I cannot. All I can recall is starting to feel dizzy and faint. Obviously, I had passed out and hit the left side of my face on the corner wall.

Against all advice, and my own better judgement, I still go in to work. I do not want to miss a scheduled training. When I walk in the office, my boss takes one look at my face and insists I leave right away and go take care of my injuries. I end up on my back in a hospital gown at St Thomas' Hospital Accident & Emergency unit. What are the odds?

Tests are run, x-rays are taken, and anti-inflammatory drugs and a drip are administered through my veins. I am told that low blood pressure might have contributed to the fatigue and the fainting that I experienced. The results of the x-ray show damage to my facial bone and I am referred to see a cranial surgeon.

What started as, and should have been, a normal day sees me spending time in an accident and emergency unit. I take two days off work to heal before returning to work. I really feel like things are spiralling out of control.

Two Days to Reflect

Those two days give me time to think. I am sick, and I am tired. My life isn't shaping up the way I expected or wanted it to. I am sick and tired of:

- Having someone else dictate how I spend my time
- Being assigned tasks and given deadlines within which to complete them.
- Having my employer 'approve' my holidays or time off based on when it is convenient for them.
- Feeling guilty for not being able to spend quality time with family and friends.
- Not having as much time as I would like to pour into my children and to shape them for the challenges of life.
- My social life being almost non-existent because I am either too busy or too exhausted to spend time with friends and family.
- Feeling unwell, of experiencing constant pain in my shoulders, neck, back, and waist.
- Excruciating, stress-induced headaches and blinding migraines that make me want to lie down and never wake up.
- Taking days off from work, not to rest - no, but to attend doctors' appointments and school events.
- Feeling brain-dead and irritable when I get home after a hard day's work followed by a long commute home.
- Enduring a long, boring commute to and from work, and quite often not getting a seat on the crowded rush hour trains.
- Huffing, puffing, and running for the train only to be left standing on the cold platform as it pulls away.
- Constantly feeling rushed off my feet to the point where I feel like my brain is full of nothing but clutter.
- Sleeping late and waking early, and being sleep-deprived to the point where my memory starts to suffer.

- Feeling pulled in all directions – work, family life, and my dreams, with no time to pay attention to myself.
- My love life suffering because I get home from work severely exhausted and unable to properly engage with my partner.
- Telling myself I have a great day job when I would rather be somewhere else doing my dream job.
- Feeling diminished, demotivated, and inconsequential.
- Sitting in the confinement of a 9 to 5 arrangement when I want to be changing lives and making the world a better place.
- Feeling resentful because my day job prevents me from unleashing my big, bold, audacious dreams upon the world.

I'm not sick and tired because my job is horrible. On the contrary, my job is respectable, my salary is good, my work environment is nice, my colleagues are decent and hardworking folk, and my bosses are friendly and relatable.

The underlying reason for my dissatisfaction is that I know I have a mandate of purpose upon me. I can literally feel my time running out with each day that passes. My job pays the bills, but it does not take care of everything, and I know this to be true of most people in paid employment.

I dream of doing work that I am passionate about doing, which resonates with my inner core on a deeper level, and which allows me to make more income while working fewer hours. I want that work to enable me to amplify my voice, extend my influence, and impact the lives of others by sharing my message on a global platform. My 9 to 5 is definitely not the work I dream of doing.

It is time to move on from earning an income in the confined way I am currently doing. It is time for me to break free of my self-imposed prison and escape my 9 to 5. I write this book as my invitation to you to join me in my escape.

The Decision to Plan the Escape

For far too long, I have been sitting encamped at my mountain of discontent while time ticks away. I have been watching the hourglass run out and then lethargically reaching over to turn it around so that it can start its course all over again. I do not see that I have a choice. My mountain seems so huge it seems literally insurmountable. It is too high to climb over and too wide to walk around. With so many demands on my time, I am too exhausted to even try.

My time is not mine to use as I desire. It is being paid for by my employer, and he who pays the piper gets to dictate the tune. I have practiced and perfected the dance steps to accompany the tune, and it seemed to serve its purpose for a good part of my adult life. Now though, I am starting to resent being forced to dance to someone else's tune.

There are days when the boss says to do ballet, and I want to do the cha-cha or the conga. This stifles my creative spirit. My internal vision of myself as a leader rejects the idea of being dictated to on a day-to-day basis and taking orders. I realise I can pick a darned good tune myself. I desperately want to pick my own tune.

My newfound realization leads me to struggle with the idea of having a boss dictate the tune. I want to pick my own tunes. Feeling diminished by the situation leads me to finally admit to myself that this is no longer working for me. There is no position in my company that will allow me to become what I desire to be, or to serve the world in the manner I was born to. To reach my full potential, I must escape and become self-employed.

It is time to conquer my mountain. It is time for me to stand in my truth and walk in my personal power. I feel a sense of urgency to connect with my purpose that nags me non-stop, giving me no peace or respite. It becomes my obsession.

I do not simply hand in my resignation and leave. I am not ready yet. I don't want to break out too soon only to find myself quickly recaptured and back in the prison. I know I need a plan — an intelligent and deliberate plan.

Discovering the Shine Factor and the Shine Zone

My 'eureka' moment comes the day I clearly receive two revelatory phrases in my spirit: "Shine Zone" and "Shine Factor." I know that my future endeavours will take shape from these words and the concepts they represent in my mind and spirit.

My Shine Factor is that personal brilliance that only I can offer the world. It's an activity, passion, endeavour, or enterprise where excelling comes easily and naturally to me.

Once I identify my Shine Factor, it is time to relocate to my Shine Zone. My Shine Zone is that special, unique place or 'sweet spot' where I can effortlessly bedazzle and inspire the world to greatness by just by being me. I am building my plan around those two concepts.

Coping with Confinement

Planning my escape is difficult while in the 9 to 5 prison. I work for an investment management firm. My daily interaction is with technical data, graphs, technical legislation, and regulations. These are the type of documents where you have to read and digest voluminous amounts of data to find that one paragraph that pertains to you. On a day to day basis, making the switch from my 9 to 5 logical-analytical persona to my 5-9 creative persona is not easy.

Many times, I don't succeed in making the mental switch until late Sunday evening. Sundays bring the stress of knowing that, in only a few hours, Monday will come to interrupt my creative flow. I dread the thought of waking up, getting dressed, and dragging myself into work just so I can continue to bring in the much-needed bacon.

Creativity becomes my only respite. Whatever spare time I can find, and it isn't much, I spend writing. At first, I find myself writing only rhymes, toasts, lyrics, and limericks. I write whatever comes to mind, not caring about the rhyme or rhythm of it.

Those creative efforts are my therapy, something I do to keep myself sane. They feed my creative persona and help me stay true to my core. I call them my creativity shots, and like a junkie, I find myself craving them.

I would wake up very early in the morning and head straight to my home office to get my fix before setting off to work each day. Entering into that creative space makes it easy to forget all about everything. Nothing else matters, not even eating or showering.

I push myself at a punishing pace. I give myself no time to rest, recuperate, or sleep. When my body complains, I silence it. There is far too much to do, so much to accomplish, and only 24 hours in which to get it all done.

I did dream of writing a book, but at the time I didn't feel it was something I could do. I thought it would take too much sustained effort. With my energy levels so low and my attention span so short, I believed my brain was too exhausted for that. It took meeting Dr. Ava Eagle Brown, the author of the Foreword of this book, to change my perspective on that.

The Growing Disconnect

While I sit in containment each day, I notice individuals who are out there already doing what I want to do. They are boldly pursuing their dreams, and I admire them. They are not seeking anyone's permission to live the life of their dreams, and they are not waiting to be hit by a perfect, "money back guarantee" idea. I chose to interview them, and those interviews are woven throughout these pages.

Each of them started on their journey, tentative and imperfect, but failing forward. They make mistakes, pick themselves up, and move ever forward. They are facing up to their fears, defeating their demons, and refusing to give away their voices. They are determined to show up and to speak up. And the world is taking notice.

The more I learn about them, the more I yearn to follow them to freedom. I want to be doing what they are doing. I want to be out there doing goose-bump inducing stuff to influence and impact my world. Instead, I sit confined in a corporate cubicle, playing small while pretending to be great.

The more I listen to them, the more clearly I see that my desire to make an impact on and influence the world on a far larger scale cannot be contained in a brick-and-mortar corporate establishment. I want to birth my dreams, build an empire, and create my own establishment. I want to be 'the example' and 'the poster child', but I am doing none of those things.

My inner frustration at the disconnect between the life I want to be living and the life I am living is huge. I see my 9 to 5 as a huge chasm that stands between my best self and me. It stifles my desires and prevents me from doing what I must do in order to do what I truly want to be doing. I realize what I need is a 'Perspective Punch', something to help me see things in a whole new way. It is my dreaded daily commute that provides that perspective punch.

Sitting in Limitation Limbo

Despite seeing others doing what I want to do, and despite knowing I am meant for more, I sit in my limitation. I am, like most people, a creature of habit. I feel hemmed in by my circumstances. I feel confined, restricted, and imprisoned. I am desperate, like I am suffocating, and eager for escape.

My daily commute is filled with dead energy. Everyone is crammed onto the cars like cattle waiting for slaughter. Each one buries their head in a book, newspaper, or mobile phone with earphones plugged firmly into their ears. It makes the long commutes unbearable.

Sadly, I don't know what to do to get off the conveyer belt. The thoughts I entertain of leaving feel like an act of betrayal. I can't justify leaving behind what is a very respectable and well-paying job with a certain and secure income to drag my family through the insecurities of pursuing my happily ever after life.

I commute this way for years until one day I find myself standing on a stuffy, tightly-packed morning rush hour train. I am nestled uncomfortably beneath the smelly armpit of a fellow commuter who appears in need of a bath. As I look around at the deadbeat, vacant faces of the disgruntled rat race crowd, I experience a sudden moment of clarity. A quiet thought comes to me.

"This must be what it feels like to be in prison. Someone else is in charge and in control of your time and your activities. You are compelled to jump when they say so."

That thought is immediately followed by another.

"I'm better than this. I'm more than this. Why am I stuck in this rut of mediocrity? Why am I stuck in this vicious cycle of averageness, this conveyor-belt of a 9-5 that offers no opportunity to express the real me? I'm called to be more, to do more than this. I need to get out. I need to answer that the deeper call. I need to start living."

I know, with utmost certainty, that I am not meant to run this rat race much longer. I can't spend the rest of my life feeling like a puppet on a string or a hamster on a wheel.

The Mental Battle

I am a practical person. While alluring images of liberation continually play in my head, my sensible, realistic mind counters by offering up its wise counsel, free of charge, without being asked. It reminds me repeatedly that stability is paramount.

"Don't do anything stupid that you would regret. Do you know how many people would love to be in your position, have your kind of job in the city? What's this pre-occupation with a grand dream of changing the world? Focus on changing your family's fortunes by continuing to earn a good and steady income."

My family means a great deal to me. I want to give them the very best of me. I married and started a family in my late 30's. My children are only 6 and 8 years of age, still quite young, and they rightly feel entitled to my attention. It is not enough to help bring in my share of the bacon. I need to also be available to them. To add to that, I feel I also owe a duty to my family back home. They rely on me.

The mental lectures do not end there. My rational persona is intellectual, sensible, and unrelenting in reminding me of my great job. It continually assures me it would be foolish to rock the boat. The reasons it presents for maintaining the status quo are very 'valid'. It continues scolding me.

"If God wanted you to pursue these fantastic dreams and ideas, you would still be unmarried, and you would not then have to factor family obligations into the equation. Let sleeping dogs lie. A bird in the hand is worth two in the bush. What you want won't come cheap; it would mean huge investments in time, money and focus – which you can't afford. Don't try to fix what isn't broken. Move on with your life. Forget it. It can't be done. End of story."

My visceral persona is quieter in her promptings, but no less convincing. She reminds me that I need to be true to myself and walk in my truth. I love my visceral persona. I connect with her on a deeper, gut level. I feel her in my core, and I want to be faithful to her and heed her promptings.

I am becoming quite familiar with and accustomed to my visceral persona. I often feel like an umpire-referee as I watch and listen to my rational persona do fierce battle with my visceral persona. They are at cross-purposes.

I continue going with the flow even though the tide is not flowing in the direction I want it to go because staying with the flow means certainty and security. It means my family and I remain protected from the prospect of a loss of income if I dare give up my day job and go in search of my dream job.

There are times when my dreams feel like a tall order, a fantasy that will never come true. I am caught in the middle of a career crisis, unsure of how to get out of the corporate prison in which I find myself.

Satisfaction, true joy, and fulfilment elude me. I am not living out my life's purpose, and every day brings with it the self-criticism as I walk in to work with my shoulders bowed, feeling worn out from the commute. Every day I ask myself the same questions:

"What are you doing still sitting here? What's holding you back? Why can't you move on?"

I become like Jekyll and Hyde, with a multiple personality disorder of sorts, in the sense that many people around me value my opinion and benefit from my good counsel, yet I feel unable to help myself.

I feel like I'm riding a treadmill, and I can't see how to stop the treadmill or how to get off it. I feel helpless, as the treadmill spins out of control. It makes me dizzy, while demanding that I run faster and harder. I try to keep up with it, like a hamster on a wheel.

I feel like a wind-up toy, the kind you'd wind up and place on the floor and watch as they scampered around, mindlessly and without direction, until they'd run themselves out of steam and stop unceremoniously.

That's pretty much how my life feels on a good day. On a bad day, I still feel like that wind-up toy, only broken. When these wind-up toys malfunction, you wind them up and place them on the floor as normal, but rather than move, they stand in the same spot and make the same whirring noise they did when they were working. But they don't move. They remain in one spot, all sound, and no movement. That is how my life feels.

I move between feeling a fear of going to my grave without answering my call to feeling sorry for myself because I feel there is no choice for me, and then on to judging myself quite harshly for lacking the ability to "just do it."

Why can't I just quit my job like many 'strong' women around me seem to be doing? I encounter many women who tell me, 'I just got fed up, and I quit!' I look at them with awe and envy, concluding that they are made of 'sterner stuff' or that their circumstances are different from mine.

I eventually come to understand that it will take a complete re-programming of the mind and a very deliberate re-learning process. I know what I want - to stop exchanging my time for money, to gain greater time freedom, along with Impact, Influence, and Income. But how to go from where I am to where I want to be? That is the real question.

"Fear can be very persuasive. Don't let it talk you out of walking in your power and living your best life!" - Clara Rufai

---

As I begin to search for those answers, I meet Sami Grosse, and an idea begins to form in my mind of steps that I can begin taking to make my escape.

Meet Sami Grosse

Samantha 'Sami' Grosse works part-time as an Emergency Unit Coordinator at a local trauma centre. In her free time, she is a health and wellness coach, fitness instructor, model, and event staffing manager. As a self-described bookworm, adrenaline junkie, fitness enthusiast, and world traveller, Sami's interests are as diverse as her experiences.

Her first job was at age 15 replacing the secretary of a physical therapy clinic for three weeks while the woman went on vacation. At 17, she worked as a technical support representative at the National Call Center for KFC for two years. She might never have gotten where she is today, however, if it weren't for everything that happened to her at age 19.

She began struggling in school, and was eventually diagnosed with anxiety disorder. A teacher at school told her she would never get back into college because of her academic difficulties. She became afraid of failure because it would prove her doubters right. She was equally afraid of success because she would have to maintain the success or improve on it.

She made a decision, though, not to let those fears hold her back. She began forcing herself to confront her anxieties head-on rather than running from them. She began modelling to confront her anxieties about being in front of a camera. She walked on a catwalk for the L'Oreal Redkin hair show to confront her anxiety about social embarrassment.

She went back to school despite her anxieties about her past performance and got her International Event and Wedding Planning Professional certification and her AEC in Event Planning and Management. She is working on her DEC in psychology, getting licensed as an NLP practitioner, and is finishing her certification as a Fitness Instructor Specialist. She interned at a hospital on a pilot project for patients with early signs of Alzheimer's and Dementia and with Dawson Community Centre's after school program for adolescents. She graduates at the end of the school year.

Planning Her Escape

She moved from her job at the National Call Center to working in Admitting at the trauma centre. Working at the hospital was not a typical 9-5 job. She worked for the provincial government, which meant job security, benefits, and insurance.

She tried working a full-time day shift but between the fact that she is not a natural morning person and her micromanaging boss who picked on everything except her actual work, she soon decided that was not for her. She realized this was not something she could see herself doing for the next 27 years of her life.

She couldn't move up without a medical degree, which she was not interested in obtaining, and feared moving to another position would bore her after working in the most stimulating department in the hospital.

Further, the position required her to work weekends and holidays. She got tired of missing out on events with friends and family members. Although she never knew what might come through the doors during a shift, her work was fairly repetitive. Rather than leaving the job to pursue her dreams, she decided to work part-time evenings instead.

Freelance modelling, event staffing gigs, coordinating events, and doing the odd gig now and then as an extra sparked her interest in entrepreneurship. Owning her own business appeals to her because it gives her more freedom to pursue her interests, to make an impact on the world, and to plan her day while allowing her to give back to her community by sharing her story of pursuing options outside of living a conventional life while being part of helping people to prevent chronic and avoidable conditions that rob people of their vitality.

It is also more fun. She can pursue the things that interest her, meet amazing people, and get paid better than she is now to do it.

To give her more time to pursue her interests, she moved from working full-time to working part-time evenings at her position. Sami finds the corporate world very constrictive. She couldn't seem to find a position that allowed her to pursue her interests and paid well. She didn't like having her day planned for her. Sami also did not like having to follow rules that didn't make sense because "things have always been done that way." The conventional rules of life never appealed to her free spirited nature.

Sami's amazing sport coaches taught her so much about life, hard work, teamwork, striving for excellence, and recovering after a loss. Their help inspired her to want to make a difference by helping people to see options they may never have considered while giving back to the community.

While her full-time coaching practice is still a dream, she is already taking on clients. Her current plan is to launch her website while she works on getting more one-on-one clients before adding group and intensive sessions.

Her long-term goal is to grow a life coaching business that prioritizes health and wellness for living a fulfilling life. She intends to serve 18-45 year olds that want to make healthier lifestyle habits a priority, seek more adventure in their lives, and support those who struggle with self-doubt due to anxiety.

She helps her clients explore their options, recognize and find ways around their limiting beliefs, empowering them to take charge of their lives and see that they are capable of achieving more than they thought they could. Her strategy is to focus on companies that offer wellness programs to their employees.

While working toward her goal, she intends to get involved on the committee overseeing the wellness program for her current employer and then apply that experience to other companies. Eventually, she intends to write a book.

Like me, Sami is waiting for the right time before making her escape, but while she's waiting, she's actively putting together her route and gathering her resources as she develops the resilience and focuses on the reasons why all the work is worth it.

Sami's Lessons on the Run

1. Find supportive and like-minded people if those closest to you are not.
2. Put yourself out there - it's the only way to get feedback to make adjustments if needed.
3. When you first start, keep it simple. Get clients and use your personal network. All the marketing info can be overwhelming and isn't a priority at the beginning.

Connecting With Sami

Website: www.crawfordcoaching.ca

Facebook page: www.facebook.com/sami.crawfordcoahing

Instagram: www.instagram.com/crawfordcoaching

LinkedIn: https://ca.linkedin.com/in/samigrosse

Liberation's Call and the 4 R's

Meeting Sami confirms for me what I want above all else: freedom of time and location. I want to run my own business, working on my own terms and at my own pace, all while achieving impact, influence, and income. I need to liberate myself from the containment of my 9 to 5 in order to do that.

I possess a strong character and emotional toughness. I have always seen myself as a leader. Leading people out of mind-set prisons is something that attracts me. However, after months of burning inside with a message to help people break free of their limitations, I still sit in chains.

To break this conundrum, I know I must challenge the status quo and be intentional about breaking apart the chains that bind me. To help me think through all that I need to do in order to break free, I began to look at my situation as if it were a true prison. What do I need to do in order to make good my escape?

First, I must figure out what my Shine Factor is and where my Shine Zone is located so that when I do escape, I escape into a life that will be worth all the work it will take to get there.

Second, I need to decide why I am breaking free. I need a REASON compelling enough to keep me going any time that I am tempted to quit or to give in when the inevitable difficulties come my way. I need to remember why the work I am doing is worth the pain I am going through to get the results I desire.

Third, I need to map an escape ROUTE. Choosing a route for escape means knowing where all the pitfalls and the obstacles are and having a plan in place for getting around each of them. Until I have a clear idea of what awaits me, I won't know what resources I need to gather, and I won't know how to develop the kind of resilience I will need to face what's coming.

Fourth, once I've drafted my route I need to gather my RESOURCES. Those resources are financial, mental, emotional, spiritual, and physical. Financial resources act as a parachute to help me clear the gaps. Mental resources involve developing the right perspective to get me through tough times and challenges I am sure to face.

Emotional resources include putting together a support team to lean on when times get tough and to help keep me focused ever forward toward my goal. Spiritual resources, such as meditation, keep me grounded in something greater than myself when I am afraid to take the final leap from limitation to liberation. Physical resources mean learning to take better care of my health so I can maintain my focus and endurance while I'm on the run.

Fifth, I need to develop RESILIENCE. No plan, no matter how good, is going to survive meeting up with reality. Resilience allows me to make changes to the plan as I go, adapt to unforeseen circumstances, and make the best of things when nothing goes the way I intended it to go.

Chapter 2:
Finding My Shine Factor

Finding my Shine Factor is a journey of self-realization. It requires me to ask questions of myself and to give honest responses. The goal is to find my purpose, that thing I was born to do.

I love how my friend, Brandy M. Miller, puts it in her essay, "Why Are You Working So Hard?"

"You've been taught all your life that you must work hard in order to achieve great things. You've never questioned that. You've seen examples of it. You've seen people who have built great wealth by working hard.

But what you've not seen is the pain that they experienced getting that wealth. What you didn't see is that they reached the top of the pyramid, looked down, and asked themselves, *"Is this all there is? Is this what I've worked so hard to get?"*

They reached success the hard way and it felt empty to them. They didn't experience the feelings of fulfilment and satisfaction they expected. They didn't like the life they'd built for themselves. Yes, they were comfortable - but they felt trapped by the comfort. They were dependent on keeping it going because they were afraid of what would happen if they let go of it all.

Here's the truth: Water does not have to work hard to flow. The only time water has trouble flowing is when there is something standing in the way blocking it.

Figure out where you flow. Find what comes naturally to you. Work in that space. That space is where you will come alive. That space is where work becomes play and you will want to spend all day doing what you do because you can't imagine doing anything that feels as good to you as this does.

If you don't feel eager, energized, and excited by the work you are doing, then, that work is not meant for you. Connect with someone who does feel that way about the work and allow them to share their gift with you as you share your gifts with them. Don't be a prosperity dam by holding back your flow from reaching others because you're afraid to trust yourself to them."

> *"Let yourself stay in your flow and make it grow by allowing others to contribute out of their flow." - Brandy M. Miller*

Mindset Matters: Who Am I?

> *"Success consists of several battles fought and won over a period of time. Once you win the battle of the mind, the entire war is as good as won."* - *Clara Rufai*

Let's talk a little bit about self-perception. How do you see yourself? Forget who or what others say you are. Who do YOU say you are? How you see yourself matters significantly and is the singular most important factor to your success. Of course, success depends on a host of factors, but if I were hard-pressed to choose just one, this would be it – mind-set. This is the key driver for success.

Personally, I could not have made it out of the many woods of my life if I did not have mental toughness. Mental toughness and a sense of 'unbreakability' have been crucial in seeing me through. This is also my secret strategy for coping with a pressured and busy lifestyle.

One of my goals is to equip you with mind-set tools that will enable you to break free from your place of containment, free you from every prison that holds you bound, and to live your best life. In other words, exhibit your 'Shine Factor.'

That being said, in this next section, I would like to give you a sneak peek (it is by no means an exhaustive list!) into my mental rhetoric and how I perceive myself. I call them my 'I AM's.' The letters I, A and M have deeper meanings to me as follows:

I - Internal Rhetoric

A - Achievement Potential

M - Meaningful Progress

I strongly believe that changing our internal rhetoric (our inner script) increases our achievement potential (our ability to aspire, to dream and to do the work to bring our dreams to reality), thereby enabling or leading us to make meaningful progress in life! I have found this simple but meaningful insight to be quite motivational - and you should try it too!

When I ask "Who am I?" single, one-word answers such as "lawyer" or high-fallutin' expressions such as "Investment Management Professional" do not suffice.

Over time, I compile a list of the answers I give in response to the question, "Who Am I?" These become my "I AM" statements which I use to remind myself of my identity when I am feeling badgered by my rational persona or discouraged about how long it is taking to assemble my escape plan.

I AM:

1. <u>My Father's Daughter</u>

I am my Father's daughter. This is a statement I make with utmost pride as well as with a sense of responsibility. My father was a man whose actions were guided by a heart of love, understanding, and concern for the wellbeing of others.

It was not until after his death that we became aware of the full extent of his generosity and philanthropy. People would come to tell us about the good things he had done for them while he was alive. He had done all of them in secrecy, not even my mom was aware. For instance, we heard how he had single-handedly purchased the Listre Power Generator Plant for the church in our hometown.

It was said that he'd bought the Power Generator Plant for his personal use in our compound but then decided it was unthinkable that he should have light in his compound while his Father's house, referring to the church, was in darkness.

He gave the generator to the church, saying that the same God that has provided that one will provide another for his personal use. That was not his only philanthropic deed for this church or others.

Countless many others benefited from his kindness, too. Growing up, a regular feature or high mark was sharing bales of clothes, wrappers, and other goodies to people. One aspect of his philanthropy that we did know about was the distribution of largess to family and outsiders during festivities like Christmas or Easter, partly because we were part of the planning or were logistically co-opted as 'food soldiers' to deliver the sundry items to people. There were numerous other acts of selflessness and generosity which we only came to know about after my dad passed away.

Today, I often joke to close friends that my husband and I run an unregistered charity. We take very seriously our self-imposed responsibility to help others survive in the face of hardship. Today, generosity and serving others has become part of my character. I can say this without apology or false modesty because I know it to be the truth. - I cannot sleep easy while someone suffers. For this reason, I can never understand or respect the inordinate flaunting of wealth in a world where so many still suffer.

I AM:

2. <u>A Reed</u>

Despite the constant feeling of being so rushed off my feet, and so stretched to the breaking point, I have come to discover, "Oh wow, I'm NOT going to break, because I AM A REED."

A reed may be tossed and blown by all kinds of adverse winds, it may bow or bend in the varied storms of life, but it never breaks. Resilience and staying power are a part of its nature. Survival is in its DNA. When the storm passes, a reed has the ability to bounce right back and still stand. I AM A REED.

I can identify with the nature and the character of the reed! Let me explain: The reed is a grass-like plant that is both resilient and resourceful. Its various species have proven useful to man for generations:

- The giant reed is used for making musical instruments
- The paper reed or papyrus was the source of ancient Egyptian writing material and is also used for making boats
- The common reed (also known as the thatching reed) is used for thatching roofs

One plant, so many uses, all because of its resourcefulness and resilience - and that is how I choose to think of myself as I journey through life. I never, for one moment, allow myself to doubt the fact that I have an unbreakable spirit within.

My predominant thought always is and always will be *'I am born to conquer.'* This is what inspired me to write this journal note to inspire and encourage myself one fine Saturday in October 2015:

MY INNER GAME STATEMENT

I AM

BORN

TO

CONQUER!

Your inner game allows you to stand out, to look different and to show that difference boldly. Trust your inner fabric - always!

I AM:

3. Born To Conquer (BTC)

What's in a name?

> *"This is a name that captures and encapsulates my belief system, my life's philosophy and my guiding principle towards life and life's issues."*

It is my unshakeable belief that no matter what life throws at me, I will always overcome because it is hard-wired into my genes and DNA to always CONQUER. This is not negotiable. I do not permit my psyche to doubt it even for one minute.

There's strength of character and strong will that I believe God in His wisdom lovingly and deliberately wove into my character when He made me. I have simply resolved to make Him proud by being true to who He, my Master, created me to be.

I can go on and on. I can carry on writing, because BTC means a whole lot to me. It represents so much more than just a name. *Born To Conquer* is my ideology. It is my belief. It is my way of life. It is my life's calling. It is my posture. It represents my positioning.

I am more than a conqueror.

I am Clara Rufai - born to conquer

I AM:

4. <u>Tenaciously-resilient</u>

Now I should mention that this mind-set, my conviction that nothing life can throw at me will ever break me, is a choice I deliberately made. I made this mind-set choice and reinforced it over and over during some of the lowest points and darkest periods of my life.

The one thing that is universal in life, besides death, is pain. Pain does not discriminate. It happens to all of us regardless of age, gender, or colour. We all experience pain at some point in our lives. I am a strong believer in the clichéd saying that *'what doesn't kill you can only make you stronger.'*

All of our life's experiences, the good, the bad and the ugly - including the pain - combine to mould us into who we are or who we eventually become. They are all useful tools and should be seen as such.

While pain and hurt have, sadly, been known to alter many people's course in life, I have come to understand through my own experiences that the moment in which we learn or choose to see our life experiences as learning tools is the moment that pain and hurt lose their stranglehold on our lives.

I am no stranger to pain and I have had my fair share dished out to me in life. Yet, today, with the benefit of hindsight, I see clearly how those painful moments prepared my body, mind, and spirit for the rest of my life.

I have not always known this, and truth be told, it took me a long time to learn this lesson. However, I can certainly testify that coming to this realisation lifted a heavy load off my then young shoulders, after I lost two younger siblings in a boat accident.

I AM:

5. <u>The Real ME</u>

The real ME is creative, expressive, and poetic. The real ME is always excited when adding value to others. The real ME wants to mentor, to teach, to coach and to inspire others into becoming the best versions of themselves.

What Do I Want?

I know who I am. In many ways, I already know what I want and what I do not want. I create a checklist of things I want and things I do not want. When opportunities come, I can compare them against this list to be sure they are aligned with my passions.

It is easier, and more obvious, to first answer the question "What don't you want?" I know I do not want to die in my 9 to 5 prison. I know I do not want to die unsung with no evidence that the world can point to and say, *"This is what she left us, this is what she birthed."*

Here is what I do want. I want to die emptied out and poured out into the world. I want to do more, be more, achieve more, show up more, lead more, and teach more. I want to be more than what I am. I want to speak my mind, share my voice, change lives, and make the world a better place. I want my impact to be way bigger than myself.

I want to do work that nourishes my mind and tends my soul. I want to answer that primal call within me to touch lives and add value globally, not just locally. I want to be out there, doing goose-bump inducing stuff. I want to be 'the example' and 'the poster child.'

I also want to give my family the best of me. I want to be free to spend quality time with them. I want to stop exchanging my time for money so that I can gain greater time freedom, and increase three things - impact, influence, and income.

I want to participate in grand speaking engagements worldwide, on stages big and small. I believe very much in the power of technology and social media and I want to leverage them to create a six figure income doing stuff that I enjoy doing.

My Opportunity Checklist

1. Will it allow me to do more than I've done before?
2. Will it push me to be more than I am now?
3. Will it give me an opportunity to show up more than I am currently doing?
4. Will it allow me to lead more?
5. Will it allow me to teach more?
6. Will it allow me to influence others?
7. Will it allow me to impact others?
8. Will it allow me to increase my income?
9. Will it allow me to speak my mind?
10. Will it allow me to share my voice?
11. Will it allow me to impact my world?
12. Will it nourish my mind?
13. Will it tend my soul?
14. Will it touch lives?
15. Will it add value globally and not just locally?
16. Will it make the world a better place?
17. Will it make me feel fulfilled?
18. Will it allow me to continue giving the best of myself to my family?
19. Will it allow me to have freedom of time and location?
20. Will it open doors to speaking engagements?
21. Will it allow me to leverage social media?
22. Will it be something I will enjoy doing?

What Are My Talents?

As a child, I was always a creative soul. My flair and interests always leaned more towards the arts rather than towards the sciences. At college, I did effortlessly well in the more creative and expressive subjects such as English Language, Oral English, and Literature in English. I struggled with the 'drier', more technical subjects such as Mathematics, Chemistry, and Physics.

I was drawn to speaking in front of others and acting in drama. I was active in the school's Press, Debating, and Drama clubs, all early manifestations of my creative and expressive personality.

In my younger days, I also showed a keen interest in and a great aptitude for writing, acting, and speaking. The interest still remains today.

What Are My Gifts?

I am born to lead. All my life, even when I did not actively put my hand up or seek it out, leadership opportunities have been laid upon me. To my family, I am the reliable, strong, and optimistic one. To my friends, I can be counted upon to lead, to bring order, and to carry people along. I know all of these things about myself, but I had never before sat down to synergise these thoughts and observations. I had never asked myself what they meant, or what they could mean, until recently.

My opinion is valued and sought after by many, and being a positive influence in other people's lives also comes naturally to me. I am great at inspiring and supporting others while they birth their dreams. I am excellent at helping other people gain clarity and resolve their issues.

What Do I Enjoy Doing?

When it came time to choose a career path, I recall being very keen on studying theatre arts at university but my family did not think it was a good idea.

"What would you do afterwards, how would you make a living on that?"

Given my love for English Language and Literature in English, I have always enjoyed playing with words. I love writing poems, rhymes, limericks and short pieces to inspire. I also enjoy business coaching, mentoring, and inspiring others.

What Experiences Do I Bring?

Part of my Shine Factor is the life experiences that I bring to life's table. Every single one of my experiences is useful and can be deployed to help me understand, connect with, and communicate to the audience I will be serving. They give me instant rapport and 'relatability' and empathy because those I serve will know that I understand what they are going through because I speak their language. This will prove priceless to me in building faithful followers and captivated clients.

If it seems negative to dwell on past hurts and failures, I do this for a reason. I do not believe that there are any negative experiences in life, only negative perspectives that we can bring to those experiences.

The things that hurt us most cause us to grow in our ability to help others heal. It is not how we are hurt that matters but what we do to heal from it that gives us the strength and compassion needed to offer encouragement to others who are going through that same pain.

The failures that we experience are our greatest teachers. They offer us invaluable lessons that we can then use to build toward the success we desire. Failure is nothing more than a learning opportunity in disguise.

My experience inventory process looks at the things that have hurt me in the past and what I did to heal from those wounds, the failures I've experienced and what I learned from them, the achievements I've accomplished and what those affirmed for me, and the struggles I've overcome to get where I am today and how I did it. I discover that the process familiarises me with myself in many respects.

Hurt 1. My Father's Death

I grew up in the south-eastern part of Nigeria, in the oil-rich riverine area. Ours was a large but close-knit family, one in which cousins related more like brothers and sisters. As far back as

I can recall, my dad was that incorruptible and respected man who stood for justice and he would give the very clothes on his back to make someone else happy and comfortable. Dad was a born a philanthropist, an altruist and generous to a fault. His selfless philanthropy and generosity touched lives far and wide.

When I was 13 years old, my hero, my father, died – this is the earliest shock to my system that I can recall. However, it was not to be the only shock as I was to discover later. What made it so shocking was because to my child-like mind, my dad was just too good to die young - his life was a blessing through and through to everyone he encountered.

His death was a rude shock not just to his immediate family, but also to the entire community as he was benefactor to many. His philanthropy was well known and widely talked about in the entire village.

HEALING: I heal those wounds by choosing to continue his legacy of caring for others and serving their needs to the best of my ability.

Hurt 2. Being Discouraged from Pursuing My purpose

When I expressed a desire to pursue theatre arts in college, those who loved me and wanted 'the best' for me discouraged me. That led me down a path to becoming a lawyer, which was a very dignified and respectable career that they were sure would bring me success in life. They thought a degree in law was a great choice for me.

HEALING: I am healing by working towards getting back to doing what I was born to do.

Hurt 3. The Loss of My Teenaged Sisters In a Boating Accident

Ten years after my father's death, my two younger sisters drowned when the ferry that was carrying them across a creek capsized. There was a little rain, some wind and flashes of thunder before the boat carrying them across tipped over.

Survivors told us of a discussion between the girls, as they stood waiting to board the nearly-full boat that day. We were told that one of the girls had not wanted to board the overloaded boat. She suggested they await the boat's return so that they could go in the next trip across the creek. The other girl had suggested that wasn't a good idea as it had started to rain by that time – an unexpected, churlish rain – and they were fast getting wet.

Neither girl had swimming skills, but we gathered that Ibifuro had managed to make it to shore or close to shore, when she heard her younger sister Ibinabo calling out for her help. Without thinking, Ibifuro went back into the river to try to save her sister. They both drowned. It was the saddest day of my life!

I could not understand why these two angels should die so young, and I also struggled to reconcile the manner of their death!

There were 19 people on board, most of them school children. Of those 19, only four of them were able to be rescued. My sisters were not among those four. We were fortunate that searchers were able to locate their bodies so that we could give them a burial. However, it was not the sort of burial that I would have wanted for them. Their bodies were found the day after the incident, fished out of the creek, mutilated, eaten by fish and crabs.

I was not there at the time but I have often wondered how my mom was able to cope with the sight of her daughters fished out of the cold, muddy waters of that creek.

As is the custom, such mutilated bodies must not be brought onshore into the community. Their bodies were therefore left at the waterside, in the boat in which they were picked up, covered up with fronds or mangrove leaves or cloth - I don't know which. It is at the waterside that anyone emotionally able to behold the sight would go and to catch a glimpse of the corpses. I do not know till this day whether or not my Mum went to look at the bodies of her daughters – it is a question I have never asked her. It is a memory I am eager to spare her. I want to completely undo and erase it if it were possible.

I remember clearly my Aunt breaking the news to me. I cannot recall the exact words she used but I remember staring at her blankly, then as it sunk in, I stared at her in shock like she was sprouting a second head on her neck. For a few painfully long minutes I waited for her to tell me she was joking, that it wasn't true.

'She had to be joking' I thought. God would never allow such a terrible thing to happen to us, after our family suffered the loss of our patriarch and breadwinner at a time when we still needed him. His sudden death had left us in confusion but we had survived it.

These deaths were even more shocking and more painful to me. I recall going through life in a hazy daze during the months that followed. I was distracted and dejected and questioned why I should carry on living. I still struggle to remember portions of my life during the years that followed my sisters' death.

I nearly ran myself mad during the years afterward, often wondering how my mum would cope with having to carry on living in the same house where she'd grown used to seeing, feeling and hearing her two young, carefree girls. How did she deal with the absence of their hugs and their laughter? How did she live without hearing their voices? Oh how the silence of the suddenly quiet house must have taunted her!

So many thoughts plagued me. How did she manage to the task of emptying the house of all of their personal effects? What did she do with their personal effects? Did she burn them? Did she give them away?

Then my mind would stray to my sisters and I would wonder about their last hours minutes alive. I would torture myself thinking about how they died. I would vividly feel their fear as they struggled to stay afloat. My eyes often widened in fear as theirs must have done in those final moments when they realised they were going down, down, and down for the final time.

I grew very familiar with a potpourri of feelings - guilt, fear, despair, anger, self-pity - as they often mixed themselves together into a repugnant melee of emotions. I cried so much my eyes often felt hot and gritty, like I had grains of fine sand in them. My throat perpetually ached, constricted and hardened with unshed tears.

I felt miserable and quite sorry for myself. My helplessness and the finality of the situation often led me to break down without warning and in the most unexpected of places.

Ironically, it was during those days, in that dark place of festering sorrow and hopelessness that I discovered and developed my resilient persona and my irrepressible spirit. Faced with two options, I made a choice to conquer, to overcome, and to thrive. I refused to consider any other option.

HEALING: As part of healing from that major hurt and for the sake of my mother and my sisters, I decided I would find a way to not only survive but to thrive and to one day share their story so their lives would not be forgotten.

Failure 1. Allowing Others to Choose My Path

When my family wanted me to become a lawyer in spite of my desire to pursue theatre arts, I was young and felt I had no voice and no say. I went along with what my family thought to be the best choice for me - a degree in Law. The rest is water under the bridge as they say.

I often wonder how my life might have turned out, had I gone ahead to study theatre arts like I had wanted. One thing is for sure - I would have ended up with stellar grades because my spirit would have been in total alignment with my passion throughout the 4 years of studying for my degree.

That level of interest and engagement would have ensured that I thoroughly enjoyed my time at university. This is what I refer to as *'passion-alignment'*—when your passion is in perfect alignment with your actions, leading to ease and enjoyment. This is what I define as the 'Shine Zone'. It is only in this 'Shine Zone' that we get to meet the best version of ourselves.

I believe that if I had studied my course of choice, I might never have gone into the corporate world. Had I gone ahead to study for a degree in Theatre Arts, that would naturally have led me into coaching, speaking, mentoring, and inspiring others to live fully and purposefully. But that was not the way things turned out.

LEARNING: What I learned from that failure is that choosing a path outside your purpose is a recipe for dissatisfaction in life, no matter how much fame and fortune it promises you.

Failure 2. Staying Too Long in a Life Not Meant for Me

After completing my degree, I went on to the Law School in Lagos Nigeria, which was like a sort of 'finishing school' for graduates of law in the country. By this time, I already saw myself as a respectable lawyer and my future seemed pretty set to follow on nicely. I went on to complete the compulsory government-imposed National Youth Service Corps programme.

Once I finished the NYSC induction period, I went on to work at a small law firm in the Northern part of Nigeria, in fulfilment of the work placement requirement of the programme. Upon completing the compulsory programme, I relocated back to Lagos, the then capital city of Nigeria, where I did a short stint with a small law firm before setting my sights on a career in the banking industry.

The banking and oil and gas sectors promised much better salary structures and so a majority of new graduates desired those 'lucrative' jobs. I succeeded in gaining employment into one of the largest and most established banking institutions in Nigeria, where I proceeded to serve a 'prison sentence' of 13 years as a member of the bank's sizeable legal team, before resigning in 2006 as an Assistant Manager.

Thinking back on my 13 years at the bank, I can truthfully say that for at least 10 of those years, I was dissatisfied, frustrated and even borderline-depressed. I recall the 'sameness' of things there, the monotony of life, the mundaneness of it all, the woeful bleating and complaining, and the constant hope for change which never came.

All of this led me to silence the many voices playing in my head that attempted to call me out to something greater. It all seemed not just impossible, but if it was possible, I concluded it was far too much work. It was far easier to simply 'maintain the status quo' and 'go with the flow.'

Slowly but surely the years rolled off of each other, until one day, suddenly (not!) I woke up to find myself a 'veteran employee' having sat in the same unsatisfactory job for more than a decade. Why? How? Well, it's easy - anyone can do it. In fact, the vast majority of people do it year after year, some until they go to their graves.

I was too scared and lacked the direction to change the status quo of sitting in confinement, in a role I was not passionate about. Also, every time a fellow 'inmate' was released early (when the bank declared redundancies) I heaved a sigh of relief at having missed the cull. Along with hundreds of other 'inmates,' I empathised with those 'inmates' who had been set free from prison.

I deliberately use this powerful imagery because I know that some colleagues who were laid off went on to use their severance pay to set up entrepreneurial endeavours that were more in line with their passions. Many of them reported being more at peace, enjoying life more and feeling more fulfilled. This proves the point that although many of us go through life maintaining the status quo; the greatest achievements often come from boldly questioning and disrupting the status quo.

I often wonder: what if I'd had the courage and the motivation all those years, to grant audience to my entrepreneurial yearnings? What if I had pursued my dreams rather than sitting in limbo? What if I had started something that resonated with my core and aligned with who I knew I was on the inside? Perhaps I may today have been enjoying the same fame as the originators of

Uber or AirBnB – as they all started out with an idea. Anything is possible when you believe in yourself.

LEARNING: What I learned from that is that the longer you stay in a life not meant for you, the harder it becomes to leave.

Failure 3. Failing to Speak Up for Myself and My Dreams

Not speaking up for myself and my dreams not only led me to a different career path than I might have chosen, it had me sitting in limbo far too long. This is despite knowing that I was headed down a different trajectory than what I wanted. As I got older, I wanted to do whatever I could to 'get back on track', to embrace my calling and to walk my own path. The lag between decision point and the point of what I might call full implementation left me feeling quite trapped and impatient. I was so anxious that I developed a nervous stutter. This carried over to other areas of my life.

I went from being one of the most confident 'debaters' at secondary school to being hesitant in my speech. Whenever I tried to speak, my words would climb and trip all over themselves. I would find myself going blank mid-sentence as I tried to remember the next word(s) to finish off my sentence.

At work, I could see the look of impatience on the faces of my colleagues when it seemed like I took longer to finish off my sentences. I began struggling with my confidence. Socially, though I continued to appear confident and self-assured, I became hesitant to speak up even in the small groups and networks to which I belonged. The more agitated and I was, the more this became a self-fulfilling prophecy. Soon, I developed a 'signature lisp' that refused to go away.

LEARNING: I have learned from that failure is that no one takes your voice from you; you lose it because you fail to use it. Once people get used to not hearing you speak up, they eventually forget your voice. That's how you 'lose' your voice.

Failure 4. <u>**Pushing Myself Too Hard and Neglecting My Health**</u>

I told you earlier about my fainting spell. However, that is not the only episode I have experienced as a consequence of pushing myself too hard. I will share one funny episode with you. It is funny now, but it gave me quite a scare at the time.

'Where's my hat? Has anyone seen my hat?!'

I mutter these words under my breath. My question is directed at no one in particular. I have searched frantically for my winter hat for a good ten minutes while keeping the family waiting. We were getting ready to leave home for an appointment and were already running late. If only I could find my hat!

It was winter and far too cold to venture out without proper protection against the elements. The rest of the family was all kitted up and ready to head out the door. They waited while I searched, not really paying me full attention at first. After a while, my husband asks with some irritation.

"What's keeping us? If we don't leave now, we'll be late!"

My then 7-year-old notices I am searching for something and decides to help.

"Mummy, what are you looking for?"

His question irritates me. I am in a hurry and feel impatient.

"My HAT! I'm trying to find my winter hat, son. I can't go out without my hat - it's quite cold out there!"

My son looks both perplexed and a little bit amused.

"B-but Mummy, your hat is on your head!"

I feel quite embarrassed.

"Oh?"

My hand instinctively flies to my head to confirm my son's assertion. Sure enough, there my hat sits, perched on my head. I have no recollection of putting it on, even though I must have done so only moments before.

I am a little miffed at myself. I kept everyone waiting while I embarked on a manhunt for a hat that wasn't missing! I apologise for keeping my family waiting and there is some laughter and banter made about it as we finally get in the car and drive off.

All through the 45-minute drive to our appointment, I cannot stop thinking about the incident. After diverse episodes of forgetfulness occur, I admit to myself what is quite obvious: I am sleep-deprived, exhausted, and distracted - at least, I hope that's all it is. My brain seems to be atrophying from stress and sleep deprivation. I start to struggle to maintain focus, especially at work.

A niggling concern begins to grow within me. Soon, the niggling concern turns to morbid fear. I begin worrying that something might be seriously wrong. What if I have a tumour or something growing in my brain? Severe anxiety sets in, with panic following closely in its wake. I quickly book an appointment to see a Neurologist who specialises in cognitive disorders, dementia, and stroke. I insist on undergoing an MRI scan.

Waiting for the test results is more than a little scary. My mind plays all manner of tricks on me and fear torments me. After a torturous week of waiting, the results of the scan come out rather 'inconclusive.'. However, this only super-sizes my fear. Finding nothing obviously wrong on the face of it, I am referred to yet another specialist who takes me through a series of tests that include tests to check my motor skills, hand-eye coordination, deductive and observation abilities. Suffice to say that I don't perform as well as the specialist and I might would have expected, given my educational qualifications and literacy levels.

Expressing some surprise at my 'poor' performance, the specialist concludes that I am overworked and under-rested. I need to relax as I clearly have too much on my plate. She has a stern discussion with me about my daily routine which she thinks 'seems quite stressful.'

When I mention my desire to embark on a Ph.D. programme, the specialist looks at me with undisguised concern and some consternation. Her reply is, however, calm and quiet.

"I would not recommend that at all, Mrs. Rufai. You need to take things off your plate, not put more on."

LEARNING: What I learned from that is that denying my body of what it needs to do its best work in order to get my dreams and goals accomplished is a lot like denying your car the needed maintenance and repair work because you're in a big hurry to get to your dream awesome vacation: it is not likely to end well.

Failure 5. Missing out on Quality Time With My Boys' By Being Too Busy

It is not unusual for me to return from my day job and, although completely exhausted, head straight upstairs to my home office to carry on working on my 'escape agenda.' I am determined to craft, fine-tune, and implement my Escape Agenda. Unfortunately, this translates to less time spent interacting with my family. One evening, soon after I walk in from my day job, I had to hurry to join a training conference call.

My 6-year old keeps coming in the room, indicating he needs my attention. I can see the plea in his eyes but I want to finish my call. I keep silently gesturing while on the conference line, letting him know it is past his bedtime, and that he needs to go to bed.

Finally, an hour and a half later, I finish my training call. By this time, the boys overshot their bedtime by almost 2 hours. I can still hear them downstairs talking loudly and excitedly when they should have long been in bed. My stress levels begin to build.

"Why are you boys still awake? You should have been in bed two hours ago!"

I give them my signature, disapproving glare and herd them from the living room to their bedroom, and start tucking them into bed. As I lean in to kiss my 6-year old goodnight, I want to reassure him that even though he has disrespected his bedtime rules, I still love him.

"Mummy loves you very much son, but you must learn to respect bedtime; sleep is very important for little boys to grow up strong and smart. You know that don't you?"

My little boy's responds in a small but deliberate voice.

"Mummy, I just wanted to tell you that I was very good at school today. I did really good work and my teacher moved my name tag up one notch - I even got a star badge and a certificate too. I put them in your room on your dressing table for you to see, Mummy."

Instant guilt washes over me. My boy wants to make me happy and proud by sharing his successes, but I am too busy trying to achieve my own success to pay attention to his. He has achieved so much in the course of his school day, and he just wants to share with Mum.

I apologise to my precious lad. We kiss and make up. As I tuck him into bed, he says something that touches my heart: "It's okay, Mummy. I know you're busy, and I still love you." I love my little boy so much in that moment.

I hate being too busy to spend quality time with my children. Like most Mums, I want to be front row and centre-stage in my children's upbringing, I want to be their chief educator, and their first sounding board.

LEARNING: What I learned from this is that I need to find a better way, one that does not require me to choose between my job and livelihood on the one hand and my family and life fulfilment on the other.

Achievement 1. Winning the prize for 'The Best Actress in the School'

One of my proudest accomplishments in my secondary school days was being awarded Mr S.K Olayemi's prize for The Best Actress In The School. This affirmed me in my desire to be on stage and in my passion for calling to the theatre arts. I narrowly missed out on the prize for 'The Best Literature Student in the

School', which was a bitter disappointment for me, but that I came so close to winning it also affirmed me in my ability to write.

Achievement 2. Employment at the Largest & Most Respected Bank in Nigeria

Nothing can take from me the sense of accomplishment at having won a position during my banking career. It was a highly coveted spot, I set it as my goal and achieved it. That recognition affirmed for me the fact that any goal I desire I can achieve if I am willing to put in the work to achieve it.

Achievement 3. Promotion to Assistant Manager

Being promoted to Assistant Manager at that same bank affirmed for me my leadership potential. It showed me very early on that I have what it takes to manage a team.

Achievement 4. Finishing My First Book

There is no feeling quite like having finished my first book. This is in spite all the odds stacked against me to get it done. I am able to hold the final product in my hands and say to the world, "I did this!" This affirms me in my ability to write. It also affirmed the power of my story to make a difference.

Achievement 5. Appearing on Televison

Finishing my book led me to being invited to appear on a TV show. It is one of my dreams come true to have been able to speak in front of so many. It was a privilege to be able to inspire others who feel trapped by their 9 to 5 to consider alternative possibilities and coping strategies. This affirmed me in my decision to write, as a way of amplifying my voice.

Struggle 1. Dealing with My Resentment

Normally, I am a very grateful person. However, while speaking with one of my coaches, she made me realise and admit how I could unwittingly be jeopardising my own chances of success. She forced me to embark on a 'Be grateful on purpose' exercise. Over a period of 7 days, she challenged me to look inward and around me for things to be deliberately grateful for, including my 9 to 5.

By focusing on reasons to find gratitude for even the things I do not want or like, I am able to overcome the resentment of feeling stuck in limbo and instead to see my day job as funding my transition to my dream job.

Struggle 2. Managing My Time Better

My attempts to get off the 9 to 5 treadmill often leave me feeling dizzy as it spins out of control. It seems to demand I run faster and harder until I am out of breath and it feels as if my chest will explode. I often feel like I am being attacked left, right, and centre by a myriad of obligations, with no time for myself. I am seriously sleep deprived as I try to get done everything I need, as quickly as possible.

To overcome this constant feeling of being in a time crunch, I learn to prioritize the projects in my life according to my priorities, eliminate the activities that are not in alignment or which can be stopped temporarily. I constantly aim to reduce those that cannot be eliminated, to make the most of small pockets of time. This gives me more time to get projects completed so that I can enjoy the process the process of growth. It also enriches my journey.

Struggle 3. Overcoming My Mindset Limitations

Escaping my mental prison involves a deliberate resetting and rewiring of my thoughts, habits, and beliefs. I recognise that my mind is my most powerful asset. I celebrate the fact that I am mentally strong. My mind is the compass that shows me which direction my life is headed. The compass does not lie. If I do not like the direction my mind is heading, I need to change my perspective.

To help me overcome my mindset limitations, I develop a series of Perspective Posturing Statements and Re-Posturing Exercises. These help me keep myself positive and accountable no matter how negative the situation may seem.

Struggle 4. Figuring Out How to Create my Escape Agenda

One thing that I struggled with, which I'm sure is also a source of struggle for many, is not knowing how to create the change I desire. Think of a rusted screw and bolt where the bolt is rusty from being stuck in the screw for a long time. The rust welds the screw and bolt together, making it difficult to extract.

Preparation is required before the bolt can be safely and successfully removed. Proper tools, such as a vice grip, pliers and socket wrench, may be required. You may need to first spray the screw with a penetrating catalyst to loosen the rust in order to successfully separate them.

It is no different when it comes to unscrewing yourself from the bolt of your day job and transitioning to your dream job. The rust of life, such as habits, a fixed mind set, self-limiting beliefs, fear, doubt, worry, uncertainty, ignorance, lack of clarity, and perhaps also a bit of indolence, get in the way.

In creating my escape agenda, I am doing a lot of preparatory work on myself – a case of Learn Before You Leap. It is a never-ending journey of self-improvement and development. I am here to announce to you that you will have to do the same too if you are serious about moving to your place of personal brilliance.

My Education

The last piece of the puzzle is my education. This includes any training, certifications, degrees, or other credentials I have acquired along the way that lend credibility to my work. I am a lawyer, a compliance professional, and an investment management professional.

Taking a thorough inventory of what I can offer to potential clients is a good beginning, but I need help translating it all into a 'Shine Factor Statement' that will make sense to the people I am interested in serving. For help with that, I turn to Brandy for her assistance in putting it all together. It's one of her many specialties.

Meet Brandy M. Miller

Brandy is a Creativity Consultant and Writing Coach. She helps people find their unique message, identify the audience it is best suited to serve, and then figure out how, when, and where to deliver that message for its greatest impact on that audience.

It wasn't always that way. Here is her story:

She was a hot mess. No joke. She won't hide that fact from you. She is 40 years old and runs a business of her own, but she is certainly not living the high life. She usually gravitates between scraping by the skin of her teeth to being just a little bit over comfortable. Some people might think that makes her unqualified to serve people and teach them.

However, it is her being a hot mess that makes her qualified to help people embrace their vulnerabilities and turn what most people would count as a negative into the greatest positive of their lives. She likes to say that the only thing that separates a positive from a negative is the line we use to divide it.

She was a nineteen-year-old mother and made such a mess of that situation that at age 7, two months before his 8th birthday, her son stood in her bedroom telling her not only that he was going to kill himself, but exactly how. And he had a backup plan ready in case that first plan failed.

All her life, she had dreamed of being a wife, a mother, an entrepreneur, and a great saint. And here was proof staring her in the eyes telling her that she was failing miserably at two of those four goals. Her marriage was a train wreck, too. All the businesses that she had ever tried to start ended in colossal disaster.

That moment was a turning point for her. She realized that if she didn't figure her stuff out right away, she was going to lose everything that ever mattered to her. She had a choice to make. Life or Death? It was that simple.

It's been 13 years since that awful day. I'm happy to say that her life is a very different one today than it was then. Her son is 20-years-old, has a good head on his shoulders, and is making his way in the world.

Her marriage to her husband is a true partnership and she is eternally grateful for his presence in her life. She owns her own business and although the financial struggles are real, what she does is important and satisfying work. She loves it so much she would gladly do it for free and sometimes still does.

She is no great saint yet, but will be one day. She'll be the 'Patron Saint of the Undecided' helping those who feel lost and are afraid to commit to finding their path and the courage they need to make that commitment.

While she will admit that she is a hot mess and always will be, that mess is what gives her a message of hope, healing, and of finding joy and humour in the darkest of dark days. It's her greatest asset.

To all her fellow hot messes out there, she encourages you to step up, step out of the shadows, and let yourself be seen. The only thing you'll lose is your shame, your guilt, and your fear. Not a bad bargain!

Planning the Escape

She spent 26 years in customer service and sales service environments, then spent two years working in a marketing department of a Fortune 500 company. She thought she was ready to go it on her own because she was sure that she knew what marketing was.

She started her own company and fell flat on her face. Marketing with a $0 budget was a completely different experience from marketing with $5000 and an established list of customers. She spent the next 5 years learning branding and marketing the hard way and realized that your story is your brand because in your story is your message and the ideal audience that message is best suited to serve.

She has lived in Texas, Mississippi, Wyoming, and Nevada working in retail, medical, religious, legal, hospitality, publishing, and IT sectors throughout he career.

She worked in more than a few 9-5 jobs. The challenge was that she never felt like she was using all of her skills, talents, and knowledge to serve and never really felt like she belonged to any of those places. She always felt like she was meant for something more. She simply lacked the courage and – she thought - the money to get out there and start her own business. What she really lacked was the commitment to her dreams.

Life After the Escape

She made the transition to owning a business of her own painfully. Brandy was following her husband's dream of being in radio and got to a small town where her only choices for employment were to work minimum wage jobs or to step up and use her gifts. Her husband's connections at the radio station connected her to her first client, but she didn't know how to grow the business.

She didn't know how to get new clients. That struggle to learn how to get new clients took her along a path toward developing her writing talents and making it the focus of her business and serving other writers in her community. What she learned along the way is that growing a business bigger than ever before begins with serving others more than ever before.

It is in serving others that she discovered her talents for strategic analysis and creative synergy, talents that she now uses to help her clients figure out how to get more, do more, and serve more with their gifts than they thought possible with less effort and time than they could on their own.

Brandy's Lessons on the Run

Her advice is non-traditional, but it serves her well, so she is passing it along to you:

1. **Make love the foundation of your business and you will never go wrong.** Love is the one thing everyone needs and nobody else is giving. Build love into your brand and you will have people eager to get whatever you have to offer.
2. **Seek to serve, not to be served.** Serve not from a position of seeking to gain but out of a sincere desire to help them and you will build a reputation that gets people coming to you rather than you chasing them. Serve and the success will follow.
3. **Pray daily for the clients you had, the clients you have, and the clients you want to have.** Prayer marks an

intention to serve, that intention will get you listening for opportunities to serve the people on that list, and will put you in position to be ready to serve when that chance does come along. It's like watering the ground before planting the seed - it softens the ground to be ready to receive the seed when the time comes to plant it.

4. **Don't assume you know all the answers** - each person you meet holds a portion of the truth inside of them. If you assume you know it all, you won't be ready to receive that portion when it comes your way. If, however, you are aware that you don't have the portion of truth that they do, you'll be open to receiving the wisdom that only they can give you because only they have the unique combination of life experience, skills, and knowledge to offer.

5. **Know why you're doing this.** That 'why' needs to be stronger than money and that 'why' has got to be powerful enough to keep you going when you feel like curling up into ball and dying or lighting up a match and torching everything. That 'why' is what gives you the wings to fly past the things that stand in your way.

> *Corporations expect their employees to compartmentalize themselves. You are expected to bring only a portion; the portion they want, to work every day, and to leave behind the portion they don't want. Human beings weren't meant to live that way. Integration is important. Integration is the key to integrity – Brandy M. Miller*

Brandy was not born to live according to the status quo. She was born to stand out and live large. She was born to make a difference, not blend in or fit in or be like everyone else. She believes that stories are the key to connecting people at a deeper level. They are the key to creating world peace. Once you know someone's story, you fall in love with that person, just the way you fall in love with the main character in a book.

By growing her business, she is contributing to writing the world a better place. A business of helping people step out of the shadows and into the limelight by being authentically and truly themselves so they can bring love and light to a world in darkness. Her goal is to serve creative entrepreneurs and the people who teach them by showing them how to make the transition from living in fear to understanding just how much power they have and make a difference in other people's lives just by being themselves.

It only takes changing one person's life for the better to change the entire course of human history. By helping others to make a difference, she is exponentially increasing her power to create the world she wants for herself, her children, and her grandchildren.

Moving Into the Future

Brandy is currently in the process of launching a new program called Doing Business in America where she will be interviewing small business owners and sharing their stories with aspiring entrepreneurs. Her intention is to provide free exposure to the business owners and free success education to the entrepreneurs.

Over the next 18 months, she is also planning a live event in Las Vegas called "Writing the World a Better Place." It is a thought leadership seminar for writing instructors and English teachers where she shows them how powerful their work is in its ability to impact lives far beyond their individual students. It will be held January 13-15th, 2018 - Martin Luther King, Jr. Holiday weekend.

During the next 3-5 years, she is working on developing a 40-Day Writer Reality Television series where 40 writers will compete over 40 days to finish, polish, and pitch their manuscripts to publishers who then compete, Shark Tank style, for the rights to publish it. She wants people to see what it takes to bring an idea from concept to publication.

Connect with Brandy

Email: 40daywriter@gmail.com

Twitter @WriterBrandy

Facebook: https://www.facebook.com/BrandyMMiller1975

Website: http://40daywriter.com

Discovering My Shine Factor

With Brandy's help, I am able to finally put together my Shine Factor Statement.

"I provide leadership mentoring of aspiring coaches, corporate professionals, and disadvantaged youth through writing, speaking, and acting so they can learn to express themselves, find the confidence to make their voices heard, and present themselves in a way that is both entertaining and inspiring to others."

Armed with my Shine Factor, it is time to figure out where my Shine Zone is and how to begin relocating there so I can begin making the difference in the world I know I am born to make.

"The people who are crazy enough to think they can change the world, are the ones who do." – Steve Jobs

---

Chapter 3:
Locating My Shine Zone

My Shine Factor Statement is what I have to offer others. Now I must figure out where I can offer it that will make it truly useful. I must find that place where I am Born to Conquer because what I bring is exactly what is needed for the problems my audience faces.

What Problems Does My Shine Factor Solve?

My shine factor solves three common problems: self-expression, confidence, and presentation skills. Each of these problems shows up in different ways. Those who struggle with expressing themselves don't know what to say to others. That leads them to failing to speak up, even when they have something important to say. It can mean they get overlooked, undervalued, or even overrun by those who are more expressive. It also leads to their needs and wants going unfulfilled and unmet because they aren't communicating them.

Those who lack confidence don't know their own value. That leads them to hiding their talents or gifts because they fear others won't appreciate them. It also leads them to playing small and accepting less than what they are truly worth because they don't know the value of what they offer. Lastly, it can lead to them feeling taken advantage of, unappreciated, and resentful because their inability to explain the value of what they do leads others to undervalue or even devalue their work.

Those who lack presentation skills don't know how to connect and engage with others. That leads them to avoiding social gatherings because they fear rejection. It also leads them to adopting fake personas in order to try and fit in or cover over their insecurities rather than being authentic and real about who they are. They can begin acting inappropriately out of frustration at their failed attempts or anger at the rejection they keep meeting.

Who Is Most Likely To Experience These Problems?

Asking this question made me think about where my shine zone might be and why my shine factor might be truly beneficial to others. Technical and engineering industries are most likely to experience these problems as the industry tends to draw introverts. Introverts often struggle with interpersonal relationship skills. These challenges present a barrier to employment, executive management, or entrepreneurial endeavours. They can also cause problems with interdepartmental cooperation and customer service.

What Benefit Would They Get from Working with Me?

Introverted individuals, especially corporate professionals or aspiring coaches, might want to hire me to help them overcome those challenges so they can find employment, obtain promotions, or start their own business, and achieve higher income levels.

Corporations might be willing to hire me to help their technical and engineering department staff improve interdepartmental dynamics or increase customer satisfaction so they can reduce workplace conflicts and increase customer retention.

What Would Participants Need to Learn in Order to Get the Benefits?

Participants would need to learn, as I did, how to assess their Shine Potential so they can locate their Shine Factor. Once they have their statement, they would then learn to write and deliver it to others as part of helping them learn to express themselves confidently.

What Do I Need to Create in Order to Help Them Learn?

For individuals, I need to create a Shine Factor Assessment, a Shine Factor Statement Template, and a Shine Factor Story Template. I also need to create a Shine Zone Relocation Guide to help my clients move into their Shine Zone.

For corporations, I need to create a Shine Zone Relocation Training Program that uses a "train the trainers" approach for human resource departments so that they can learn the material and pass it on to management. This ensures the corporation gets the maximum benefit from the program and offers an added value.

How Would I Deliver This Program?

With today's technology, there are a variety of ways a program like this could be delivered. I could do webinars or online training videos. I could do small group workshops or one-on-one mentoring. It's a matter of choosing what works best for me and what I think will best serve the audience I am serving.

What Concerns Must I Overcome for My Prospects?

The first concern a prospective client might have is whether or not the program will work. Releasing a test version of the program for a much smaller price than the full program will allow me to get the feedback from the people who participate to make the full program better. I will also include a guarantee that I will work with them one-on-one if they complete all the assignments and don't receive the expected results until they have achieved the promised benefits.

The second concern a prospective client might have is the expense. For individuals, I can overcome this by offering payment plans.

The third concern a prospective client might have is credibility. I can overcome that objection by posting testimonials I receive from my test clients, offering free Shine Factor Assessment calls, and conducting webinars that show what I know.

Consulting an Expert

Mapping things out this far is exciting, but to take it to the next level, I need to speak with someone who helps individuals do something like what I plan to do. I am fortunate because my coach and mentor, Dr. Ava Eagle Brown, introduces me to a woman by the name of Sonia Poleon who does this kind of work for those looking to become radio personalities.

Meet Sonia Poleon

Sonia Poleon is a Life Coach, Mentor, Business and Communications Trainer, published author of the International Best Selling Book called "The Love List," Consultant and Inspirational Speaker. She is also an entrepreneur and business start-up coach.

It hasn't always been this way because Sonia's life had a very different beginning. Continue reading and you will be taken on this roller coaster of a ride.

When her twin boys were just six years old, her husband decided the grass was greener on the other side and chose to leave after twenty-one years together. They'd been together since their early school days. It was a difficult period in her life.

He didn't actually leave straight away after dropping that bombshell. It seemed like he was also afraid to leave. By the time he was ready to leave and she'd recovered from the shock, she told him to take one of the two girls they had and one of the boys and she would take the other girl and the other boy. She didn't know how to handle four children on her own.

They both came from a housing background. She was a housing representative at the time and he was a surveyor. They knew how to play the game. She was going to remain in the house they owned and she knew if he had a girl and a boy, he would be able to get a three-bedroom property since the girls were much older than the boys and could not be expected to share a room.

He was shocked by her acceptance of his decision and her rational analysis of the situation. He expected her to be miserable and to beg him to stay as she'd done on previous occasions during trials and challenges in their marriage.

She begged him to stay because she believed, given her Christian faith, that it was the right thing to do. However, their interactions with each other completely changed. Before Sonia became a Christian, they would rip off the electric company and things of that nature. However, after she became a Christian, she chose not to do things like that anymore.

Her newfound faith changed her as a woman and a human being. She became meek, something he mistook for weakness, and he took advantage. However, she felt God was talking to her. She would pick up a Bible, open it to read, and be drawn to the scripture that says wives should submit themselves to their husbands. She would pick up another random book to read and still find a message along similar lines.

One day, when still working her 9 to 5, going to a housing agency, a certain individual came to see her at her office. Before he left, he asked her if she was a Christian and she replied that she was. About a week later, she received a book that had been left on her table in a brown paper bag. It read "Strengthen Your Marriage."

She took this to be another message from God to fix her marriage and tried her best to do everything she knew in order to try and save her marriage but things still did not get any better. For a period of four to five months, she was doing everything. He would wake her in the middle of the night to ask her to get him a drink of water. She would shut her mouth, humble herself, and get the water. Then, it moved from water to a sandwich or toast or a full -blown breakfast with bacon and everything.

Eventually, he told her that he would look after the mortgage payment. Three months later, the building manager called to tell her the mortgage had not been paid throughout that entire time. When she confronted her husband about it, he told her he had no money. She knew his income was enough to cover it. The gas bills also went unpaid, so she took back control in order to stop the bill collectors from taking everything from them.

She began to pray to God to change her husband because she knew only He could do it. Eventually she began to pray that the Lord would just make him go away from her because she no longer wanted him. Finally, the time came when he said he was leaving.

She had decided to free herself from the emotional prison and when, one weekend, he got up and told her he was leaving that weekend, her answer was, "Great!" It was a Saturday. He came by, moved his stuff, and then he was gone.

In her heart, she knew she had done everything possible to make it work, and by the time she let go, she knew there was nothing else she could have done. She was left with no regrets.

However, her husband did not take any of the children with him. All four of them were left with her.

Her ex-husband didn't pay anything to help support the children. Afterschool care was very expensive. She called her ex-husband to ask him for one hundred pounds to pay for the children's school fees. He came by the house around eleven o'clock one day and began shouting, swearing, and carrying on like a lunatic. He took the hundred pounds and threw it on the floor. He told her she had better learn to budget her money because he wasn't giving her anything else. And all of this occurred in front of their children.

She swore to herself that day she would never ever ask him for another penny, and she never did. One of the reasons he left was because he'd run up a lot of debts and couldn't afford to pay for them. It became easier for him to get out than to stay.

Things got very difficult for her, though. There were many times when she could not afford to put petrol in her car so that she could go to her job. She would walk her children to the school and then walk the 30 minutes to the station where she would bunk the train. She kept praying:

"Lord, please, don't let me get caught. I'm not doing this because I'm rebelling, I'm doing it because I'm trying to survive."

All the time her heart would be in her mouth. These were the kind of things she kept telling her children not to do and there she was doing the same things. She used to walk home from the station in tears, telling God she was tired and she couldn't do this anymore.

There was a time when she struggled to pay the most important bill, the mortgage. She had so far always managed to make sure it was paid for at all times, even if it meant they didn't have food. She knew she couldn't afford to have her family evicted. By this time, she had turned the freezer off, cleaned it out, and just left it standing there because there was nothing in it. She would tell her daughters, who were much older "Listen, we're big, we're adults. We can go without food, but we always have to make sure that the boys have got something to eat."

She thought of her siblings. Her sisters had always relied on her to do things for them. Now she was in a position where she needed them. So, one day, she took the train to her sister's house. She bawled her eyes out and was really embarrassed to admit that she had nothing to feed her kids. She put her hands over her face and was sobbing like a baby as she asked to borrow twenty pounds. Her sister brought over fifty pounds worth of groceries, gave her a lift home, and told her to let her know if she needed any help no matter what it was.

She was living from pay-check to pay-check. Her faith alone was what kept her going, but there was a day when it got too much. She didn't feel like she was living her purpose, but she didn't know what her purpose was at the time. She went to all these church conferences and her for a time she would get excited and inspired, but then when she got home, nothing would happen. There would be no change.

Planning the Escape

One day she went to a conference and the pastor suggested going to college or taking a business course. She decided right then she would go to college and turn her life around. Because she hadn't been in education for a long time, before going to college she had to spend a year researching and taking short courses in order to build up to it. She did a thirteen-week course and then a six-month course before leading up to doing her degree.

She researched the different degrees she thought she might want to do and decided that, rather than setting herself up to fail, she was just going to do something she was used to doing and that was working in housing so she went and got a housing degree.

When she told her boss she wanted to go and get her degree, he didn't understand why. He told her she had all the experience and didn't need to do it, but she knew it was her time of passion so she was serious about it. Some of her colleagues wished her luck and encouraged her because of the possibilities it would create for her.

She didn't leave straight away. But eventually, she realized it was her dream. She needed to do this for herself and not for anyone else.

During her time as a Housing Officer, Sonia remembers one tenant in particular, who held her hostage for 2 hours. He was an ex-convict who had previously spent a number of years in prison for murder. She wasn't allowed to leave the room they were in, so she sat and listened to him for two hours until he had released his frustration.

Then, there was another tenant who threatened to cut her throat from ear-to-ear, threatened to beat her with a piece of wood, and called her all kinds of racist names. These all helped when deciding to leave the job.

Life After the Escape

Sonia went to pursue her degree full time and just as after which she went on to open a children's day nursery, then a shoe shop. The shoe shop didn't flourish but the children's nursery is still going strong to this day.

Her nursery proved successful enough that people began asking her about it. That's how she ended up getting into coaching. However, her generosity got the better of her. She would give them her all and not wait for them to pay her before proceeding. As a result, her coaching business wasn't going very well.

One thing led to another and Sonia ended up being invited onto radio and television because of her reputation for helping others start their businesses. They interviewed her and asked about her portfolio of properties that she'd been building, starting with one she bought for forty-eight thousand pounds and ended up being sold for a quarter of a million pounds.

The producers noticed and liked her bubbly personality. When one of the hosts of the show needed to take time off to take care of her sick family member, they called her to fill in. She eventually worked her way into a permanent spot on air. Now she coaches people who want to get into radio and teaches them what to do to gain the publicity they desire to make their big opportunity happen for them.

She shares her story so that those who might be thinking their situation is the absolute worst and no one has had it worse than they can see that someone else has walked down that path, too. Someone probably has been in a worse situation than them, and it's the mental toughness – how strong they are on the inside – that determines their survival ability.

Sonia's Lessons on the Run

1. If you don't know what you want to do, do something. Enroll in a business course or go to college, but take some action.
2. It's your dream. You need to do this for you, not for anyone else.
3. Be ready for opportunity when it comes your way.

Connect with Sonia

Website: http://www.thelovelistbook.com/
LinkedIn: https://uk.linkedin.com/in/sonia-poleon-00922948
Twitter: @SoniaPoleon
Facebook: https://www.facebook.com/SoniaPoleonOfficial

Where Do I Go From Here?

With my Shine Zone identified and my Shine Factor located, the next step is to begin digging into the reasons I am willing to go through all the work and the struggle that is needed to make good my escape from my 9 to 5. It's time to find my why.

I am working towards the life of my dreams. . .

Line upon line, here-a-little, there-a-little - each deliberate step bringing me closer. . .

I am super excited about the direction my life is taking. Each day, I feel closer to reaching my dreams. I apprehend victory!

I look at my progress and feel a sense of excitement and anticipation. My creative powers are growing stronger every day. I am no longer a slave to perfection; I just do it!

Clara Rufai

Chapter 4:
Finding My Why

My journey to the point where I am finally willing to do whatever it takes to make my escape has not been easy. Let me share with you a little bit about the pressures and the challenges I have been through on my way to making the decision to break free. It might surprise you, but I am grateful for those pressures and challenges.

They have helped me to clarify my WHYs and became the wind beneath my wings, so to speak. They keep me fired up in my determination to escape the 9 to 5 confinement, to locate my Shine Zone, and to exhibit my Shine Factor.

Encouragement from My Sons

I am concerned about being too busy to spend quality time with my boys. I want to be part of their lives. My desire to be there for them gives me strong motivation to focus on my escape agenda. I am determined to achieve freedom of time and location.

One day, my 8-year old strolls into my home office to find me working as usual, on my 'Escape Agenda.'

I am viewing one of my animated poems when he comes in and casually asks, "Are you busy, Mum? What are you doing?' as he peers over at my computer screen. His reaction when he sees and assimilates what I am viewing on the screen is simply priceless.

"Oh wow, Mum! That says your name on it! That says Clara Rufai! Mum, you are famous! I'm soooo proud of you Mum! I'm sooo happy you're my mum!"

Enthusiasm gushes from his voice and he gives me a great big hug. He runs to fetch his brother, yelling, "Dominic! Come and see what Mummy has made! She's so cool!"

His brother rushes in to see for himself. He takes one look at the video playing on the screen, and a smile spreads across his face, too.

"Wow, Mummy, this is ultra-cool! Are you going to put that on the Internet? Does that mean you're famous now mummy?"

He looks completely impressed. This funny episode reminds me of the fact that the greatest thing I can offer my kids is to give them the opportunity to see me dream, aspire, and take action towards achieving my dreams and aspirations. By witnessing that, they will themselves be inspired to dream, aspire to, and take action towards achieving their own dreams and aspirations.

The Influence of a Parent

"Nothing has a stronger influence psychologically on their environment and especially on their children than the unlived life of the parent." – Carl Jung (Swiss Psychologist)

This statement by the renowned Carl Jung is quite profound. With certain qualifiers, I take it as a grant of permission, and a justification for a parent to live their life to the fullest and permit their children to watch them do so.

I see parents so often harbouring unfulfilled, stillborn, or truncated dreams and goals in relation to education, career opportunities, hobbies, and social or romantic relationships in the name of parenthood and its many demands. They consciously or unconsciously defer their aspirations for the sake of the family.

When a parent puts their life on hold indefinitely, when they feel unfulfilled, or long for a different life but stop themselves from going for it, this leaves them with feelings of resentment, emptiness, complacency, stress, and even hopelessness.

Children are innately empathetic and they have a way of picking this up. They may blame themselves for their parent's unhappiness.

Swiss psychologist Carl Jung believes that making such choices for the supposed benefit of our children will eventually actually harm them psychologically-which is the exact opposite of what any parent would want for their child.

As parents, we must consider all sides of the equation before we decide to use parenthood and its many demands as an excuse to not live our lives to the fullest, as God intends for us to do.

No More Playing Small

I conclude to myself, without apology, that I am done playing small. It is time for the world to hear my voice. I am going to show up, and I am going to show up filled up with every ounce of passion I possesses. I am eternally humbled and grateful for the measure of success I've received, but I want more. I am grateful for the mercy drops, but I will no longer apologize for wanting rain showers. The universe is waiting and it will give me what I ask of it.

I cannot afford to sit and wait until everything is perfect. Perfection does not exist; it is, in my opinion, the greatest self-limiting belief that exists. Flawless is a myth. Perfection and flawlessness are not only myths; they are a trait of arrogance as they fool a person into thinking that they can ever finish learning or growing. Progress, not perfection, is your strongest ally. As Winston Churchill famously said, "Perfection is paralysis. Being persistent in your pursuit of progress is far more important than aspiring to perfection."

I am ready to travel the world speaking and teaching on stages and podiums, at conferences, seminars, and summits. I'm ready to comb the highways and the byways, inspiring others to break out of the prisons that hold them bound and in confinement, to start walking in their power and living their best lives. I know it will be a wildly exhilarating and hugely fulfilling journey and I can't wait to engage with those whom I have been destined to connect with.

I am ready to welcome my future with arms wide open and live full out, unapologetic about my life, chasing my dreams with single-mindedness and with a sense of urgency, because I've come to understand that the world needs to hear MY voice and MY story and that the world will be influenced and impacted by it.

I Can Eat My Cake and Have It Too

I believe that it is possible to eat my cake and have it. I can relocate to my Shine Zone and begin to live the life I dream of living. My Shine Zone is my place of personal brilliance. It is where I feel a sense of invincibility and personal power.

I believe in democratising success. I believe that the world becomes more brilliant when each one of us attains our personal brilliance and begins to daily exhibit our Shine Factor in all that we do. This can only happen when we relocate, enter into, and start living in our Shine Zone.

Consider this: in Mathematics, 'X' is usually used to denote or represent an unknown value in mathematical equations. So a typical Math problem might say: 'If $2x + 3 = 9$, find x'.

Pretty much the same way that 'x' remains unknown in algebra, a huge amount of people are missing the 'x' in their lives. They go through life underachieving and never really connecting with the elusive 'x' of life.

Far too many of us go through life chasing after the shadows of life, while ignoring the substance of it. Sadly, a good number of us do not even know how to decipher shadow from substance, a sad reality that causes us to go around and around in unproductive and self-limiting circles, never really achieving our purpose in life.

Far too many of us go through life chasing after the shadows of life, while ignoring the substance of life. Sadly, a good number of us do not even know how to decipher shadow from substance, a sad reality that causes us to go around and around in unproductive and self-limiting circles, never really achieving our purpose in life.

Personally, my life has experienced a quantum leap since I've changed course and decided to live more tenaciously, more deliberately and more resiliently. I have been ushered into a life of abundance and greater fulfilment. Hence, my greatest desire is to show people how they can achieve the same.

As a coach, teacher and mentor, and author of this bestselling book 'Prison Break,' one of my greatest desires is to help people sort through the mess and the clutter. I help my clients sift through and separate the wheat from the chaff. I help them attain clarity around some of life's key issues, thereby enabling them to emerge into and begin living in their Shine Zone.

My Shine Factor system® teaching is premised upon the belief that as an individual, your 'x' is your place of personal brilliance. It is where shining is effortless. It is that 'sweet spot' where you not only shine, but where you shine so bright as to be declared the undisputed winner in everything you lay your hands upon. It is that place where you feel so powerful, invincible, and unstoppable that you can confidently declare 'I own my space.'

I am particularly keen on enabling start-ups and entrepreneurs who are eager to learn how they can leverage their unique edge (their Shine Factor) to build successful businesses. Let me help you find and connect with your Shine Factor. Gain Control. Get Perspective. Get Ready to Win.

Sleep Deprived

It hit me one day. I have not once managed to observe the medically recommended eight hours per night of sleep in over eight years. I also have not read much in the last 7 years. I was a voracious reader once, but then I began to experience severe attention fragmentation and a chronic inability to focus. I try my best to do some reading on the train to work, but find I am unable to focus or to assimilate what I am reading. It doesn't matter if what I am reading is a book or a newspaper, my mind can't seem to take it in and make sense of it.

It doesn't help that once I manage to find a seat on the train, I find myself dozing off from sheer fatigue. Sometimes, I find myself falling asleep while standing on the packed rushed hour train.

I've done the research on sleep deprivation. I know the drill like the back of my hand. I know that I ought to turn the computer off by 9pm, turn the lights low, and take a warm bath or enjoy a hot cup of camomile tea. I know the dangers of sleep deprivation, too.

I know it can cause balance and coordination problems, hallucinations, inability to focus, and a whole host of other problems. Yet in spite of knowing these things, I fail to follow my own good counsel. Night after night, I'm up till very late trying to figure out how to align myself with my purpose. I know, beyond a shadow of a doubt what my purpose is, but I am not living in full alignment with it. I am convinced there is a better way to do things, and this is what I am determined to find.

Orders to Rest

My fainting episode, my memory lapses, and the development of my nervous stutter led me to serious concerns about my health. I am referred back to the initial consultant neurologist to interpret the outcome of all the tests conducted. As I sit in his office, he shows me a screen image of my brain scan and gives me his eventual 'diagnosis.'

"Mrs. Rufai, I know you are convinced there's something terribly wrong, but I'm happy to tell you that, in fact, there isn't. Not from what I can see looking at the results before me. Not to downplay the symptoms and the concerns that caused you to come in to see me, but the results show that your brain is the brain of a normal female of your age. I cannot find any unusual activity going on there. Mrs Rufai, you only need to exercise personal discipline and make sure you are getting enough sleep, relaxation, and rest, as it is obvious you lead a really busy life. Do you think you can manage to do this for yourself?"

My husband, bless him, keeps telling me, "You just need to take things easy, you need to get more sleep, you need to learn to relax before you do some major harm to yourself."

His calm statement always irks me. How can I be blamed for not getting enough rest when there is so much to do? So many things need my attention, and on top of that, it really feels like the Grinch that stole Christmas is also routinely stealing some of the hours in my day. I often feel like my day has at least 4 hours less than everyone else's. I must make my escape so I can finally free up my time to rest.

Sleep deprivation is a serious problem, but then so is a life unfulfilled. Fatema Zakir, is one woman who experienced that danger first hand.

Meet Fatema

Fatema Zakir is the CEO of her own company, a nutritionist, entrepreneur, and online marketing expert who is listed among the top 10% of influencers in Singapore.

However, that wasn't always the case. She grew up believing she was not good enough. She was surrounded by negative voices and for 30 years of her life, she believed them. During all those years of self-doubt and feeling worthless, she had faith that life would be better one day. She became a preschool teacher. It was her passion to work with the kids and she loved every moment of it.

Things started to change when she became a principal, however. The passion did not last long because it became more of a business than following her passion. She felt sandwiched between the management and the teachers. The income was stagnant. She was getting raises of at most $100 per year, which wasn't even enough to keep up with inflation.

She dreamed of freedom and doing what she wanted to do. She was sick and tired of the same mundane routine, but she had no business or marketing skills and it was not in her mind to go into business for herself.

She got married at 25 looking to run away from the issues she faced in her surroundings. However, after a year of being married and struggling with misunderstandings caused by different interests, she sought a divorce. A few months after the divorce, she was almost 108 kg and that's when things began to take a turn for the worse.

That day came when she was almost immobilized by an illness that affected her spinal cord. She was in and out of the hospital four times that year, and still struggling to go to work in the meantime. There came a day when she was lying in the ambulance, seeing her parent's faces.

They looked miserable. Tears were in their eyes. There were asking her if she would ever be able to walk again. They wanted to know if she was going to be like this for the rest of her life. It scared her. She was immensely grateful for the help and support of her parents during that difficult time.

It proved to be a major turning point in her life. She turned to Google for help and began researching natural healing, nutrition, and yoga. She became active on Facebook and while searching for fan pages on nutrition, bumped into Suria Isha Sparks.

Planning the Escape

Suria was the founder of an MBA Leap Academy, a Holistic Academy where she was taught personal development, wellness and nutrition, business and marketing skills, and spirituality. Through Suria, she also met her future life coach, Siti Teeya. Siti guided her in learning about proper nutrition, health, and how to become a better leader. The two of them encouraged her to consider starting her own business.

During one of Suria's Soul Detox Sessions, she discovered that the source of her spinal cord problems was all her kept anger, frustration, worthlessness, financial insecurity, and depression after her divorce.

She quit her preschool job in September 2013 after ten years on the job. She burned the bridge behind her and left with nothing in place, no savings in hand, and the only thing that pushed her forward was her belief and faith in herself.

Life After the Escape

The next two years were difficult. She faced many struggles. She had to build herself first, get to know herself and her strengths, her passions, and her blind spots. Suria provided her with a system and the tools she needed but she was 100% responsible for applying what she was given and for making it work.

Suria also connected her with a team of other women entrepreneurs who provided help and support along the way. Rather than re-inventing the wheel to create her own product or service, she used the sales skills she was learning from Suria to make money reselling wellness products form one of the most reputable companies in Singapore and promoting Suria's programs.

It was on that team that she met and connected with her best friend, a woman who has been with her through thick and thin. Their partnership has provided her a pillar of support in developing the right mind-set and creating a routine to attain success.

It took her almost two years to get the business to the point where it could fully support her. She is still learning and growing each day. She believes in working smarter rather than harder, so she follow's Suria's advice for Effortless Success – 80% of her work is on her inner self and 20% of her work is on the actions to build her business.

During those two years, there were many moments of struggle and doubt. There were moments when she wanted to give up, times when she had no income. What kept her going was the belief in herself and the positive support around her. She was happy and could see herself a different, more confident her each day. She was making small mental shifts and learning to see life from a different perspective each day. She was striving to become more compassionate and loving to mankind.

The other thing that kept her going was the little gratitude notes that she would receive from eight of her clients who were declared cancer free. She knew she was making a difference in people's lives.

Fatema's Lessons on the Run:

1. Entrepreneurship is not about learning to make your first dollar but about reshaping your mind-
2. set to be an entrepreneur who can lead and inspire others. That is the secret to not only getting your first dollar but the billions that will fall into your lap after that.
3. Others may provide a system, but you have 100% responsibility for applying what you are given and making it work.
4. There is no need to re-invent the wheel when stepping out on your own. Find someone with a proven system or a product that sells and partner with them.
5. Put together a team to help support you as you support them.
6. Put 80% of your work on your own self-improvement and 20% into action on your business for effortless success.

7. Fall in love with yourself. You were born to life, to love, and to inspire others.
8. Believe that you can, and you will.

Moving Forward into the Future

In the next six to twelve months, she sees her business growing into Thailand and the Philippines. She also sees herself earning $10,000 monthly income in the next six months. She will be invited next year to the Harvard Business Expert Forum to speak about her journey.

Connect with Fatema

You can connect with Fatema on her Facebook page: https://www.facebook.com/fatema.zakir.16

You can also get a free 60-minute life transformation coaching from her by visiting: http://bit.ly/DiscoveryourPotential

My "Why" Statements

1. My sons deserve my best and I never want to be too busy, too drained, or too driven to give that to them.
2. My sons need to see me dream, aspire to great things, and succeed in achieving them so that they will know they can do the same.
3. I don't want to feel forced to choose between my dreams and my children.
4. I want to be part of my son's lives in a bigger way.
5. The world needs to hear MY voice and MY story and to be influenced and impacted by it.
6. I don't want to lose my voice because I'm not using it.
7. My health matters, and I need time to be able to take care of myself.
8. I don't want to feel forced to choose between my health and my dreams.
9. I don't want to die with my song still in me.

10. I want the freedom to devote myself to what makes me feel alive and passionate

LIKEABLE LIMERICKS

Start Determined

Maintain Focus

Inject Passion

Finish Big

Clara Rufai,
Jan 18, 2016

Chapter 5:
Mapping My Route

My decision to escape began with understanding and clarifying what I want, what I can offer others, and the reasons WHY I want what I want. Now I am ready to map a route to freedom. It is time to escape the limitation of the 9 to 5 prison and relocate to my palace but clarity is a first step in working my way from where I am to where I want to be. There are plenty of dangers on the way out of the prison. I need to know what those are and create plans for how I will address them.

Asking for Advice

One of my first steps forward in mapping my route is hiring Dr. Ava Eagle Brown to be my coach. She successfully made the escape and it is because of her that this book exists. In fleshing out my book, I decide to reach out and interview other escapees and get their advice on what they did, then include that advice in my book. Not only will I benefit from learning from these entrepreneurs, but my readers will, too.

Writing a book and putting it into a format that is ready for publication is no simple task, and I know I do not have time for all the work that is required to get it ready. I make the decision to invest in these things so that I can free up my time to focus on preparing my program. I decide to hire outside help to cover things like transcribing the interviews, creating the cover, formatting the manuscript, and editing.

While I work toward getting the book ready, I carry on working on my mindset. Of all the obstacles that stand between a person and successful escape, mind-set represents the greatest challenge.

A person's mind-set dictates their results. Shifting our mind-set past subtle self-sabotage and procrastination into confidence and consistent action is a proven process for overcoming resistance. The moment we shift our mind-set, we gain the momentum and the propelling power to improve our lives.

My life is experiencing quantum leaps with my decision to change course and to live more tenaciously, more deliberately and more resiliently. I am being ushered into a life of abundance and greater fulfilment. My greatest desire is to show people how they can achieve the same, and this book is my first step forward.

Interviewing Escapees

I choose nine escapees to interview. In these interviews, I hear the struggles each went through to get themselves ready and the obstacles they met along their route. This allows me to create plans in case I meet those same obstacles. Each interview reveals something new and gives me new insight. Some of these escapees I introduced you to already. Some you will soon meet.

These interviews encourage me to find my purpose and pursue it without apology. It takes a lot of courage to stand out from the crowd and follow your dreams. It takes inner strength to keep climbing when everyone else turns back.

I discover how paramount it is to understand my 'whys' and also what you want most out of life. I learn the importance of asking, "What would make life more fulfilling for you?" My answer is not the same as the next person's, and that's okay. Being different is the highest form of liberation.

I also come to discover that there are coaches specializing in practically every area you can imagine. Whether you want to ignite your passion, connect with your purpose or even discover what your purpose is, the right coach can help you get there.

The right coach can also teach you how to break through the mental blocks that are getting in the way of embracing your purpose and walking in your calling. Once you connect with your purpose and passion, the right coach can teach you how to turn your passion into profits. Just ask.

I have access to world-class coaches in various circles in which I belong, some of which I have personally consulted or worked with. Just ask and I would be happy to share my contacts, with recommendations. ASK.

Identifying Obstacles

The most common obstacle faced by the escapees I interviewed was the difficulty in shifting the mind-set from corporate employee to self-employed. It is important to recognise that there will be no one giving you directions on how to spend your time, telling me what tasks to do in order to get what you want, and in what order to do them. You will be responsible for you results. You must learn to prioritize and apportion your own time so that you are able to focus on the tasks that produce results 80% of the time and the tasks that don't 20% of the time. This can be a difficult transition.

A second most common obstacle among them was the insecurities they faced and the financial struggles they needed to overcome. Escaping the 9 to 5 means that no one will be providing you a pay check once you make the escape. There is no guarantee, no safety net, and no security except what you can create for yourself.

If you need to, you must learn how to make the sale, close the deal, and ask for the money. You must learn how to scale your business, build the systems, and put the strategies into place that will help your business grow.

The third most common obstacle was learning to sift through the advice out there on how to make things work. There is also the challenge of and developing your knowledge of yourself as you tried different things.

Each eventually learned to take their own advice, to trust in themselves, and refined their offering with each attempt. Their results are as unique as they are. Mine will be, too. This further emphasized the importance of mind-shift work and continued self-development.

12 Lessons I Have Learned on the Journey

Here are some of the lessons learned from my interviews with the escapees, and from my own life experiences.

Lesson No. 1: Have Clear Written Goals

Have clear goals and write them down. Chunk them into bite-sized bits for easier implementation. Imagine you were setting out on a trip without a destination in mind. How would you know what to pack? How would know how to get there? Or when you will arrive? Writing down your goals helps you be specific in determining what you want.

Lesson No. 2: Perspective Is Key

It's easy to get bogged down with all the available self-help information. You might be surprised at how much you can benefit from asking yourself just two questions. Be sure to give yourself honest answers. Your answers should help you determine if you're on track in reaching your goals and enable you to make an action plan that will get you there within your set timeline.

1. "If an invisible person followed you around all day, what would they see?" Would they see you wasting a lot of time? Would they see you working on your goals? Would they see someone that is just going through the motions?

2. "If you lived an average life, every day, for the next 5 years, what is the logical outcome?"

So if you kept living your average day over and over, where is your life likely to end up? Now compare that logical conclusion with the life you dream of, which you'd like to have. How close are they?

Our lives are largely the result of the actions that we take each day. Are you taking actions that move you forward to the future you desire or are you engaged in time-wasting, worthless activity? Now you can make some reasonable plans and create some good habits.

My favourite inspirational and guidance manual says this: *'Write the vision and make it plain.'*

Lesson No. 3: Trust and Obey

Trust the process. Obey your gut. Keep at it and don't sweat the small stuff. It is important to be able to tell the difference between something that really matters, and something that, in the grand scheme of things, will not affect your life in any dramatic or real way. Some of the things we worry stress and agonise about will cease to matter the next day, month or year.

Learn to delay your own gratification. Life doesn't always pay off right away so it's wise to be able to delay your own gratification. For me, this life lesson is a life-long goal that I work on each day.

Striving for success and perfection can be overwhelming. It is more important to be faithful to the process and to keep moving at what seems like a perfect pace for you. Imitating the Joneses and striving to be perfect can leave you frustrated and paralyzed.

Lesson No. 4: Expect No Approval

Do not wait to be validated by anyone. You owe that to yourself. Be your own greatest cheerleader. Believe in you. Take a chance on you each and every day. Esteem yourself highly. If you can't do that for yourself, you can't expect anyone else to do it for you.

Lesson No. 5: Ignore the Naysayers

As you plan your prison escape, you must make sure to ignore those fearful 'Franny's who will show up to offer you unsolicited counsel. They will tell you it can't be done. They will point out to you the folly of your ways and tell you it's not worth the effort. There's only one thing to do with them – ignore!

Lesson No. 6: Know Yourself, Stay True to Yourself, and Keep Moving

Life is not perfect and there is no perfect solution. Reject the lie that there is. Find your trajectory, and then design your own path, so that at the end of it all, you can say with pride, like Frank Sinatra did, "I did it my way." Be true to who you are. You'll be the happiest you can ever be when you can truly say, "I am my own man/woman."

For me, knowing yourself begins with knowing not just who you are, but also whose you are, how you got here, why you're here, what you are meant to be doing, who you are meant to be blessing, whose destiny is intertwined with yours, whose life you are called to change, who your journey partners are, what your authentic voice is, what your unique message is, who your constituency is, how to share your message, and on what platform to share it. ***This is exactly why every coach has a coach and every mentor has a mentor.***

It is perhaps safe to say that the Escape Agenda is always going to be a journey and a process as opposed to a destination, but God is good, and for each stage of our life, He releases enough insight, foresight, and hindsight for each season, enough to move you along from where you are to where He needs you to be; but never so much that you feel it is okay to disengage completely from Him and run on your own. That would be foolhardy, and it constitutes self-sabotage. I believe as created beings (sorry Big Bang theorists, you lost me on this one) we must stay tethered to our original source.

Lesson No 7: Face Off with Fear and Explore Your What-If's

What if...? Imagine for one moment that you could wake up each and every morning crystal clear and laser-eyed, with the determination to focus on the steps you know you ought to be taking to get you from where you are to where you ought to be. Well, this is not a myth - you absolutely, categorically can do so. You only need two things (1) a mind re-map and (2) a route to get there.

Lesson No. 8: Relocate and Make Good Your Escape

We are all born to shine. Every one ought to relocate and live in their Shine Zone where they can exhibit their personal brilliance. Every person who breaks out of jail must find an alternative address. You don't break out of prison and then hang around the prison courtyard, waiting to be recaptured.

The longer you sit in containment, the more crucial it is for you to have not just a plan of escape but also a plan for moving forward once you are out of the prison gates.

Let us create a mental picture for a moment, of someone who just got out of prison. Let's imagine the prison to be a confined physical space where you did not have the luxury of being able to stretch to your fullest potential.

For years, you sat contained in that confined physical space. With time, your motor skills start to feel the impact of being in that confined space, resulting in you being less fluid in your movements. You eventually resign yourself to limitations of your circumstance or condition.

On the day of your escape, you can barely contain your excitement. What do you do? Do you take off in a sprint down the road ahead? Or do you first do a stretch, test your limbs by doing a few squats, making sure your body is ready to support you?

Doing the stretch and squats is the equivalent of planning and preparing for the journey ahead. It enables you to determine your own energy levels and the pace at which you should go. One size definitely does not fit all.

Don't let the prison warden or the hangman come out and catch you, standing there, so he can handcuff you and throw you back in jail. If you must break out of prison, be sure to make good your escape. It all takes careful and deliberate pre-planning.

Lesson No. 9: Your Greatest Cheerleader Is YOU!

It is critical in life to Be-You-Do-You. This one is not to be negotiated. With so many people feeling stressed-out from the often crippling demands of modern living, self-confidence and self-esteem are truly endangered species. It can become very easy then to lie back and relax and convince ourselves that our dreams are not achievable, or that the cost of pursuing them is too high, or even that we do not have what it takes to achieve them. However, without confidence and self-worth, it is impossible to make the most of our lives.

No wonder this is now a very busy and lucrative coaching niche. There are endless depths to plumb with this niche as more people become interested in learning how to bring their A-game to the table. Even those who are already successful often seek ways to up the ante.

Do not judge yourself too harshly and dismiss yourself as not measuring up. Doubts and fears are hungry beasts, and if you give them even a tiny little bit of space, they will eat you alive. Once doubt sets in, that bed in our comfort zone quickly presents itself as a very tempting option.

Be your greatest cheerleader. Be kind to yourself. View yourself in the kindest light possible. Promote yourself to yourself as the greatest thing since sliced bread. I just love the words of my children's school motto which I have since adopted myself because it is simple, yet true and powerful:

"I can be anything I want if I can just believe in me. Indeed, YOU can be anything YOU want if YOU can just believe in YOU."

Lesson 10: Develop a Disruptor/Game Changer Mentality

Be the game changer, the world is already full of players. Don't hand out concessions just because your competitors choose to do so. You are not forced to play that game. If you must play, choose your game carefully, and play it well. Be a game changer yourself and do something different.

Lesson No. 11: Keep Building and Watch for the Ripples

Movement is key. Movement is a sister to consistency and a not-too-distant relative of momentum. Embarking on this is a journey started years earlier. I knew my course and my journey's path, but the ducks didn't come home to roost until many years later.

I sit now giving myself a 'well done you' pat on the back for not giving up, and I recall vividly all the tiny little, seemingly inconsequential steps I've taken throughout my journey. They are the reasons this book was finally birthed. Every single step combined to make this happen.

I remember years ago, being so caught up and impacted by Jack Canfield's Success Principles. I owned this great book in hard copy and audio versions. The audio version was life changing for me. It made all my tedious train journeys more bearable.

I looked forward to grabbing myself a seat on the train (if I was lucky) and just listening to that voice in my ears, re-mapping my mind, challenging my status quo, questioning my self-limiting beliefs, and opening me up to the fact that there was more. I could do more, live more and be more. I learned about fear, rejection, courage and determination, mentorship etc.

It is fair to say I was obsessed with that book because I couldn't stop listening to the audio version. That was, and it still is, the most intimate experience I have had with a book in my adult memory. Looking back now, this book gave me permission to dream again, to supersize those dreams and finally to seek out avenues of making my dreams come true.

This was just one building block, one piece of a massive puzzle, and there were many pieces. Each tiny piece was as important as its next neighbour, in that without one, the others were (evidently) incomplete and the whole picture that you see today would never have been possible.

Lesson 12. Be Authentic.

Dance to your own tune. Train your ears to shut out the noise of the construction site. Refuse to be distracted by the constant banging and drilling going on.

This is important but quickly forgotten on the day of the house warming. Learning to be authentic is not unlike the birthing process. For most women, pregnancy is tough and wreaks all kinds of havoc on the body.

Consider the discomfort of incubating that child for 9 long months. Consider the groans of labour, the pain of the push. As every woman who knows will tell you, that moment when the baby's head can be seen and the midwife tells you that only one last powerful push is required to give birth that is also the moment when the exhausted woman knows (thinks) she has no more push left in her.

It is a tough moment and the discomfort and extreme pains in her nether regions are real, but from an unknown reservoir, she manages to gather one last ounce of strength for one last push and out pops her gorgeous baby - a moment of victory for mum and baby. In that moment, all the pain seems worthwhile.

Be Watching for Opportunities

Mapping an escape route means being watchful for opportunities that open up to you. As I mentioned while discussing the process I used to find my Shine Factor, I recently took advantage of an opportunity to be interviewed on Television. Opportunity often births opportunity. That opportunity came only because my book was ready.

The closer you get to being ready, the more honed your senses will become, to notice opportunities coming your way. If you are determined to escape, you'll discover these are openings in the fence, cracks in the walls that can be widened enough to allow you to pass through them, or guards who are sympathetic to your cause and are willing to help you break free.

Sometimes these opportunities come disguised as problems, or failures. If you can solve a problem or overcome a failure for yourself, it qualifies you to then share that strategy with someone else. The bigger the problems you face, the greater the opportunities.

Develop Gratitude for Your Prison

If you can't change your prison, you can and should most certainly change how I look at your prison. You can choose gratitude, and that changes your attitude. If you have a bad attitude, are easily irritated, have no or low tolerance in general, guess what? That's not going to change when you swap your day job for your dream job. People will still be people. Stuff will still happen to test you. Life still deals you your fair share of blows. You will still get your share of life's lemons. These are unavoidable.

Life is full of various kinds of stimuli, it is how you receive, interpret and process them that make the difference.

It is your how you choose to deal with them that makes the difference. Will you be found making lemonade or whining about how 'life's a bitch'?

I spoke earlier with you about my resentment for my 9 to 5, and the work I did to find gratitude for it. When I chose to focus on gratitude, I find a certain sense of calm and equanimity as I enter my 9 to 5 space each day. I see that the people I work with are really quite a decent and hardworking bunch who are absolutely focused on delivering the best value to the clients they serve. Integrity is high on their priority list, and senior executive members are, for the large part, relatable and approachable.

I now see that where there is any form of irritation or dissatisfaction at work, I need to accept that it must be so. When it is time to move on, I should rightly start to feel some level of discomfort in my current location. It is that discomfort that acts as the fuel to propel me into the next chapter of my life. In this sense, it is a positive force and a useful energy. It actually helps my cause and course. I just have to allow it to be.

I'm indeed grateful. I'm grateful for God's love and for how He brings me into contact with those who can help me on my mind set re-set, re-programming, and re-strategizing journey. The clichéd saying, "everything happens for a reason" is really true. Changing my mind-set allows me to feel less stress coming in to work each day. I walk in with a lot more confidence and positivity.

My shoulders feel less bunched-up and less painful. I feel lighter and more in control.

I feel much happier now I have made this mind-set shift because I like my co-workers. It is important to me for me to be able to move on without any rancour or bitterness whatsoever. I do not want to destroy the hard work I've put in to build a relationship with them over the last five years.

Work Through 'What-If' Scenarios

Thinking about escaping brings up a million 'what if' scenarios. 'What if' I can't make it? 'What if' I find I don't have what it takes? 'What if' I can't bring in the income I need. 'What if' I fail? 'What if' I end up not liking what I transition into as much as I thought I would?

Rather than dodging those fears, mapping my route allows me to address them head-on and to formulate strategies for what I will do if the worst does happen. For every 'what if' scenario I can think of, I then decide to map out a correlating question. "What can I do if...?"

I have discovered on this journey that fear is not my enemy. It is there to alert me to potential dangers. I need to listen to what fear is telling me so I can be aware of where the dangers lie and make plans to avoid the traps. Listening to fear is part of learning to trust in my own intuition.

This also quiets my rational, analytical mind by letting it know that I am listening. I hear what it is saying to me about the importance of safety and security. I can then put my visceral, creative self to work finding solutions to the problems that my rational, analytical mind presents. Both sides are in alignment working to help me with my goal instead of arguing and fighting. In the end, I will be better prepared because of both sides of my mind.

There are many times when we hear that inner-voice and tend to ignore it but your inner-voice is trying to tell you something very important. If you have a strong gut instinct, follow it and trust it. Is there a big, bold move that your inner-voice is trying to call you to? Is there a trap you are about to step in to? Listen and find out.

Someone who knows more than a little about facing up to 'what if' scenarios and dealing with the difficulties involved in mapping a route is my good friend, Monique Welch.

Meet Monique Welch

Monique Welch builds and teaches online systems that allow ordinary people to earn money for their talents while having more enjoyable lives.

She is the daughter of a florist who worked incredibly hard to educate three children at university. She worked beside her mom for her entire childhood; decorating for weddings and events as well as making balloon animals and floral arrangements.

She started her first business at age 12 selling greeting cards to her customers. At 16, she pursued a career in Environmental Management and by 22, she earned a Master's Degree in Natural Resource Management.

Her first job after university was the one that made it clear that she never wanted to work for anyone for the long term. She'd just completed her Master's degree. She and her colleagues decided to bid for a project. With her educational background, she was the only one qualified to do the work and was made the Project Manager.

The contract was worth $148,000 but she was paid her regular salary of $3,000, even though they wouldn't have been able to bid for the project without her expertise. She got no additional compensation. In fact, her salary was docked an additional $200 for phone calls that were made to complete the project.

That was the last time she would let someone have total control over her income. For the three months that followed, she went to work and sat at her desk, praying that was the day she would get let go so she could use the severance money to start her hair and skincare business.

Planning the Escape

In preparation for her new business, her focus was on creating an exceptional product. She spent hours researching formulations and understanding what people were looking for that the market wasn't providing. She joined forums where her customers were hanging out and became a well-known name in that online community. As a result, when her products came out, she already had a bit of a following.

Life After the Escape

By 2010, her products became an award-winning brand in Barbados and were in the treatment rooms of some of the island's top spas. However, she got frustrated making the products by hand. Rising costs of imports eroded her profit margins, and made it difficult for her pricing to be sustainable. She wasn't making enough profit to reinvest in business growth.

At her dad's suggestion, she decided to stop and get a job. That led her to Canada, where she went to work as a spa manager. She had a 90-minute commute (each way) and worked 11-hour shifts, 6 days a week.

After a month, Monique quit her job because she was exhausted all the time. She also wanted more control of her time, she wanted to be able to travel and enjoy the money she was earning.

She wanted to be rewarded based on the results she could create and not based on some arbitrary salary that was enough to pay the bills. She would rather be broke than go through that again.

She moved back to Barbados and started a service business - no inventory and no manufacturing, so everything was great. She was selling advertising. She built a sales team and raised $75,000 in seed funding. However, the service, a smart phone app, was more advanced than the market.

Her next entrepreneurial adventure was in the creation of a dessert restaurant. It was a rocking success, but required that she and her husband spend 7 days a week at the store managing staff, restocking inventory, and processing the bank deposits.

Through building multiple businesses in a range of industries, she recognized that she had skills in branding, positioning, marketing, and web development. She began offering these to business owners. Her most recent adventure, Start Your Thing, is a podcast and community dedicated to new and aspiring people who want to begin their own entrepreneurial journey.

She works with both product and service-based business owners who wanted to monetize their talents while having the freedom to enjoy their life.

Her clients achieve incredible results. One of her favourite success stories includes a very unhappy lab assistant who quit to start a business and, by working with Monique, was able to earn double her monthly salary.

Another involves a student who participated in Monique's free 21-day business challenge and created a business, sold out of her inventory, and had back orders because she followed the steps. It's the best feeling in the world to see people living a life they are happy with and being rewarded for their talent and expertise.

She sees so many talented, creative people suffocating in a 9-5 job. They are unhappy because they aren't living a full life. They are just slaves to a pay check. Many will never earn one quarter of their earning potential as long as their employers exploit them. In some cases, they are doing work they hate while telling themselves each day that they can't earn money being creative. That makes her so sad. She has been there, but has been fortunate enough to see that there's another way early in life.

She wants everyone to know how good it feels to get paid doing the work you enjoy, be compensated fairly, and still have the freedom to enjoy the money you earn. She watched her mom work hard, sacrifice a lot, and is sad she's no longer around to share these moments with her, but there's someone out there who could have parents a little longer if they made the leap and had proper business systems in place.

Every day, she wakes up grateful for the freedom she has been able to create for her family. Her husband works three days a week and volunteers his time on a 4th day. She also gets to spend more time with him, and they get to take advantage of no crowds when they do activities on weekdays, such as indoor skydiving, archery tag, kayaking, river tubing, Segway tours, and hiking.

Moving Forward

In the next year, she'll be seeing as much of the world as possible with her husband during a 3-month road trip across Canada followed by 1 month in Italy doing Yoga Teacher certification and some other travel in between. She'll also be re-launching her skincare line and releasing an e-course to guide aspiring business owners through the steps of starting a business.

Monique's Lessons On the Run

- Before you quit, build your core business systems.
- You must know how you will let people know about you (marketing system)
- Convert conversations into sales (sales system)
- Deliver your product or service to your customer (fulfilment system)
- Manage your time, money and information (admin system)
- If you have no idea how to create and implement these systems, hire help. The sooner you have them, the faster you can generate predictable, consistent income and avoid the cash flow that most business owners end up on.

Connect with Monique

She offers you a guide to replace your pay check that you might want to take a look at - http://startyourthing.com/how-to-replace-your-paycheck/

You can join her community at www.startyourthing.com where she shares inspiring stories, business strategies and training for new and aspiring business owners.

To learn more about working privately with Monique, visit her online home at: http://moniquewelch.com/

Part II: Developing the Escape Agenda

Chapter 6:
Gathering My Resources

With my Shine Factor found, my Shine Zone located, my reasons thoroughly developed, and my route mapped, it is time to look at what resources I need to gather. I need **mental** resources to help me maintain the right perspective. I need **spiritual** resources which keep me grounded by reminding me that there is something greater at stake than my own personal happiness.

I need **emotional** resources in terms of a support team to lean on during times of difficulty or doubt. I need **physical** resources which are the development of healthy habits, such as getting enough rest, learning to eat right, and making sure that I am getting enough physical activity. Last, I need **financial** resources. These create a parachute that help me make the leap of faith from the life I am living to the life I want to live.

Creating the Mental Resource Tools

To help me with my mind-set challenges, I need tools to help me keep the right perspective on things. I create Perspective Posturing statements to recite daily. I develop Re-Posturing Exercises to use when I find myself struggling to get in the right mind-set. I also create reflection questions which I answer in my Perspective Journal to allow me to see the mental progress I am making or to spot patterns of thought that might point to a need for mental re-mapping. I call these my Perspective Punches.

Perspective Punches help me develop a proper mind-set. I recite them daily until they become my new truth. When I notice my mind resisting or telling me "that's not true" about any particular statement, I write that statement down in your Perspective Journal and use that problem area for reflection. I try to uncover why I believe it is not true, or why I am resistant to that statement.

Perspective Posturing: My Creativity Flows from ME

One of my positive traits I particularly enjoy is creativity. My creativity helps me out when I need solutions and makes my life more exciting, interesting, and fulfilling. My creativity shows in a variety of situations. It comes out when I am problem solving at home or at work. My family members also see my creativity when I am taking part in activities I enjoy in my spare time.

Co-workers comment on the unusual ways I contribute to group work projects. Many of my work associates look to me for issues that require unorthodox solutions. However, I am at my most relaxed state when I am creating something not because I have to out of compulsion but rather just because I want to out of my desire and with passion.

Whether it's focusing on a project for work, doing something fun in the garage, or simply taking some time to sketch or paint, I find that my creativity is always there for me. It is never-ending.

Sometimes, I have so many ideas that I must grab a pen and quickly write them down. I have a quiet sense of confidence in my creative abilities. I trust my judgment when it comes to creating something that people enjoy. My creativity is worthy of my time, effort, and praise.

Perspective Re-Posturing Exercise

Today, set aside time to do nothing but think creatively. With pen in hand, you can jot down the creative solutions, ideas, and artistic gems that come from within you. I am very pleased with my creativity – are you?

Reflection Questions:

1. How comfortable are you with your level of creativity?

2. Are you able to identify when your creativity is at work?

3. How can you cultivate your creative senses?

Perspective Posturing: My Dreams Are My Top Priorities

While I have many responsibilities, my dreams are always a top priority. I realize that dreams are what make life worth living. It is easy to get caught up in day-to-day responsibilities, but I always remain aware of my dreams.

I regularly schedule time to work on my dreams. They require time and attention to come to fruition. Each day, I spend at least a few minutes making my dreams become a reality. My dreams are worthy of my time.

It is easy to become side tracked, but I always remember to focus on my dreams.

At work, I use spare moments to remind myself that my dreams are important. I especially like to use the time while I am driving to reflect on my dreams. I review my goals and create plans that enable me to achieve them and you can do the same.

I surround myself with people that support and respect my dreams. Life is too short to allow other people's negativity to steal my dreams. I recognize that their attempts to discourage me are reflections of their own fears, and I use them as encouragement and fuel to remind me why it matters that I make my dreams a reality.

I create an environment that is supportive of my dreams. I am certain that my dreams are coming true.

Perspective Re-Posturing Exercise

Today, make your dreams one of your top priorities. Realize that everything else exists to support your dreams. Making your dreams come true is up to you, and you are up to the challenge. Spend 10 minutes writing or envisioning how your life will be when your dreams come true.

Reflection Questions:

1. What are your dreams?

2. What do you need to do to make your dreams become a reality?

3. What is standing in your way of making your dreams a priority?

Perspective Posturing: Everything Is Possible

The universe is vaster than anyone can comprehend. This means that there are more possibilities available to me at any moment than I could ever count. This means that anything is possible for me.

I can accomplish great things in my life and enjoy even greater achievements. The key is to recognize that anything is possible. I recite these reminders to myself each day:

- I can achieve whatever I want.
- I can have what I desire.
- I can choose any career that pleases me
- Everything is possible

I can create. I can possess. I can imagine. I can see so many possibilities and know that they are within my reach.

When I am struggling for a solution, I remind myself that everything is possible. Remembering that opens me up to discovering the solution I seek. I remember the times in the past when I found a brilliant solution to a challenge? I find strength in those memories. They encourage me to seek new solutions now.

I remember that learning to walk and talk is much more challenging than anything else I could ever want to accomplish. I learned how to walk and talk, so everything else is also possible.

Perspective Re-Posturing Exercise

Today, allow yourself to be open to new opportunities and possibilities. You are free of believing that your options are limited. Know that an elegant solution exists for every struggle you face. Know in your heart that everything is possible, and possible for you.

Reflection Questions:

1. In what areas of your life do you feel confined and out of options?

2. Can you allow yourself to believe that everything is possible?

3. How would your life and perspective change if you believed that everything is possible?

Perspective Posturing: Having Less Means More Opportunity

I am a positive thinker. I look at even the most intimidating circumstances as opportunities to come out on top. I am unlimited in my self-confidence and the knowledge that I am worthy of winning.

I embrace challenging circumstance. Sometimes, I would like to be more capable than I am, but I also know that I have what it takes to open other doors to help me achieve my goals. I am creative with my talents and can convert any circumstances to opportunity for indescribable success.

Even if I lose out on one opportunity, I can certainly prepare myself for the next. I give thanks for what I have and what I continue to receive. I know I am better off than many others and for that I am continually grateful.

I avoid taking anything that is given to me for granted. I treasure it and also share what I have with those around me.

Perspective Re-Posturing Exercise

Today, make the most of what you have. What are you grateful for? Be happy with what has been given to you because you know you have the drive and determination to use your talents and abilities to go for more. You see what you want and are committed to go after it with gusto.

Self-Reflection Questions:

1. Is it difficult for you to teach your children to be satisfied with what they have?

2. Do you share your talents and possessions with others?

3. Are there times when you are saddened because you lack sufficient resources?

Admit Your Mistakes

Every day, I encounter situations when things go differently than I hope. Sometimes, I firmly believe that what I am doing is the right thing to do. However, I sometimes choose an incorrect action. I make mistakes and that is a fact. And when I do,

I acknowledge it right away. Although it is challenging to admit to your mistakes, it is ultimately the easiest path to follow.

Any struggle I experience regarding my error is quickly relieved upon stating that I made a mistake. I am free from the stress of trying to keep the secret of my misstep. Admitting to my errors cleanses me emotionally.

I start with a clean slate when I fully accept that I made a mistake. Each day, I concentrate on doing the best I can with the knowledge that I have gained when I err. I recognize it as an opportunity to start again.

My life improves beyond measure when I recognize my personal mistakes to yourself and others. Doing this brings the freedom to go forward in life and pursue my passions. I experience feelings of renewal and hope as I admit to my errors.

Perspective Re-Posturing Exercise

Today, begin to acknowledge your mistakes. Realize it is to your benefit to do so. Learn to embrace your mistakes and to look for the valuable lessons in them.

Reflection Questions:

1. How honest and open are you in your efforts to admit your errors?

2. Do you admit to your mistakes? How does it feel? Do you admit them swiftly?

3. What can you do to be more willing to admit your errors?

Perspective Posturing: My Success Is My Responsibility

I hold the key to success in my heart, mind and soul. I embrace my inner drive and determination. It is this drive that converts my efforts into achievements. I view obstacles as only temporary pauses in obtaining the success I am destined for.

When I am confronted with a challenge, I stare it squarely in the eye. I wield my power over the challenge so it is unable to conquer me. The bravery with which I approach challenges is the tool that helps to erase any fears I may have at the onset.

Follow me on Twitter and Instagram: @clararufai

Winning is inevitable once I overcome those fears. I embrace my responsibility to ensure that each project I embark on yields positive results. I relish my role as the master of my efforts. I believe in my ability to persevere because I often experience successful outcomes after consistent effort.

Perspective Re-Posturing Exercise

Today, your success is the focal point of your day-to-day exploits. Each situation you encounter reminds you of your part in reaching your goals. Go after every goal with the mind-set that YOU deserve only the best and have what it takes to get it.

Reflection Questions:

1. How do you empower others to rely on their own abilities to turn situations around?

2. Do you remain positive if you are unable to achieve success with something?

3. When challenges seem difficult to bear, how can you allow others to help?

Perspective Posturing: Opportunities Surround Me

Making money comes easily to me. Whether I have a lot of money in my bank account right now is of little consequence, because I always have my ability to make more. There are always ways for me to make the money I desire.

I can see opportunities for building wealth in everything I do. Sometimes, opportunities to build wealth may appear small at first, but I can see how, with patience and persistence, they can become excellent money -makers.

Not all wealth-building opportunities amass a great fortune overnight and that is okay. I am open to the opportunities that surround me. Many times, the situations with the best money making potential present themselves in surprising ways, so I am ready at all times.

I look at wealth as something more than just money. I believe that true wealth is providing value to others and receiving that same value in return in whatever form of payment that it comes.

If I seek ways to build wealth, I can find it. I look to others that I admire and ask openly for guidance to help reach their level of success.

Perspective Re-Posturing Exercise:

Today, choose to seek out opportunities for building wealth. Be open to wealth in all forms and feel grateful for the many opportunities that surround you.

Reflection Questions:

1. *What forms of wealth are present in your life?*

2. *Has an unexpected opportunity ever helped to bring you wealth?*

3. *Who are some people you look up to that have achieved the level of wealth that you desire?*

Perspective Posturing: Persistence Is Important To Me

Persistence is one of my most positive character traits because it enables me to be the best person I can be. Being persistent means I gather my strength to keep doing something until I succeed. For me, it's irrelevant if accomplishing a task requires me to do it 2 times or 12 times. I keep at it until I produce the results I desire.

As I think about persistence, I realize it is important to all aspects in my life - work, home life, and personal relationships. At work, I find that persistence pays off, literally. I persist until I complete each work project in the best way I know how. For my excellent service to my company, I am rewarded handsomely.

At home, the tasks seem never-ending. But my capacity for persistence is strong. I follow through with getting home tasks done.

In managing my personal relationships, sometimes I must persist in order to enjoy the special emotional connections I have with others. I support their needs and bring them encouragement and joy, even in challenging times. I find persistence to be integral to living a quality life that provides me feelings of happiness and accomplishment.

Perspective Re-Posturing Exercise

Today, make an intention to focus on persistence. You can persist to achieve the results you want. Whether you are concentrating on your work, home or relationships, persistence is the key to your continued success. You deserve to live a wonderful life and you can persist in your efforts to accomplish all the great things you desire.

Reflection Questions:

1. How important is persistence to you?

2. Are you persistent in everything you do in work, home, and relationships?

3. What strategies can you put into place to ensure you use persistence to your best advantage?

Perspective Posturing: There Is Always A Way

I have everything I need to overcome my challenges. I am smart enough to find the solution and become more insightful with each passing day. I can create brilliant solutions that resolve my challenges as quickly and easily as possible.

My determination is the stuff of legends. I am persistent and see solutions through to completion. I laugh in the face of challenges and they soon disappear.

I am wise. I have the wisdom to determine a positive course of action regardless of the circumstances. I am highly intuitive and guided by a higher power. I am open to all the possibilities and regularly tap into my higher self. I recognize that the answers are right in front of me.

My past success in overcoming obstacles provides me with the confidence to know that I can handle new challenges as well. Challenges are learning opportunities and I welcome new knowledge. I am grateful for my challenges; they help me to grow.

I am successful, and successful people are great at finding solutions. I am pleased with my victories and look forward to many more as I conquer new challenges.

Perspective Re-Posturing Exercise

Today, get excited to be in search of a brilliant solution for a current challenge you might be facing. You can overcome any hindrance and move past it with exuberance. You are a positive force in the universe.

Reflection Questions:

1. *What is your greatest challenge right now?*

2. *What resources do you have to apply to a solution?*

3. *How can you use these resources to overcome your challenge?*

Perspective Posturing: I Am Fearless

Each day, I have many opportunities. I can go after what I want, or I can wallow in fear and anxiety and refuse to participate in my life. If I want to see my dreams come true, I must be fearless when pursuing my goals.

I am thankful that I have dreams for myself. They give me something to work for and look forward to. They shape my life with purpose and motivation. Going after what I want creates my highest vision for my life. I aim to have the best life I can.

Going after what I want in life is so satisfying. I set small goals on the way to the bigger ones and watch with pride as I achieve them. Each time I reach a goal, I grow in confidence that I can, likewise, accomplish bigger dreams. I make time to celebrate even the smallest achievements.

If I ever feel that life would be easier if I just let go of my dreams and stopped trying hard, I remind yourself that this moment is the only one I have. I only need to go after what I want in this moment. The past is gone and the future is still to come. Therefore, I choose in each moment to fearlessly pursue my goals.

Perspective Re-Posturing Exercise

Today, passionately go after the things you care about. True success means relentlessly pursuing your dreams. Love yourself and your life. Set yourself up for success as often as you can. Each day, set some small goal for yourself and then rejoice when you achieve it.

Reflection Questions:

1. Which goals are easiest for you to pursue?

2. Which goal that you would really like to accomplish seems like a pipe dream to you?

3. What is one small step you can take today toward this dream?

Perspective Posturing: I Am Free

I have choices in all situations. Nothing stands between me and my highest good. I have only to claim it, and it is mine. Being in the flow of my creative power each day is my birth right, and I am free to shape my own reality.

I trust myself to make good choices. This includes choices about my perspectives and responses. Life situations come and go, but my positivity about them is unwavering. In this way among many ways, I create my reality. At my very best, I see myself as a positive person. This highest vision of myself is manifested in each moment.

When I set my heart and mind on something, I trust that it is even now coming to pass. I have infinite co-creative power in my life. Whatever I want my reality to look like, I can manifest in abundance.

I am secure in my right to my own happiness. When a situation turns out in a way other than how I desire, I know that something better is taking its place. I am confident in this because I am constantly creating my reality and my reality is good.

My perspective on situations is always in my control, so I choose happiness and joy for myself.

Perspective Re-Posturing Exercises

Today, be confident in your own co-creative power. Use your abilities wisely. Feel free to create your own reality, so in each moment you choose to create it for your highest good.

Reflection Questions:

1. In the past year, have you successfully created a perspective that you wanted to have on a situation?

2. For you, what is the relationship between creativity and joy, bliss or freedom?

3. How do you feel when you choose to shape your reality in a way that satisfies you?

Perspective Posturing: I Have What It Takes

I am confident that anything I can conceptualize, I can achieve. I have what it takes to work towards achieving an envisioned goal. I know that with the right combination of drive, intelligence and patience, anything is attainable.

My drive and focus are strong characteristics that help turn my dreams into reality. In the forefront of my mind, I continually play the story of my life after my vision turns into reality. Imagining such a joyful future strengthens my drive and keeps me in focus. I am driven to seek ways to overcome my challenges. I feel more accomplished when I reach the end of a long and winding road and not just a mere walk in the park.

I have the smarts to make positive decisions on my way to achieving a goal. I have the intelligence to weigh my options and choose conscientiously. Above all, I exercise patience in my goal setting. In time, everything I set out to achieve is bound to be mine.

Perspective Re-Posturing Exercise

Today, look for every opportunity to use your natural talents and abilities to turn your desires and visions into reality. You can do it and with that knowledge, half the battle is already won.

Reflection Questions:

1. Do you spend time focusing on your goals?

2. How do you get yourself back on track when you suffer doubt about your ability to succeed?

3. Are challenges keeping you from reaching your goals? How can you overcome them?

Perspective Posturing: I Can Change My Results

I am a firm believer that there is always an alternative. I avoid looking at difficult situations as impossible to resolve. I can change the outcome of any situation if I change my approach to it.

I carefully weigh the pros and cons in making each decision and remain open to considering other options if the cons of my original idea outweigh the pros. I am always willing to rework my plan to achieve a more favourable result.

I am a true example of living and thinking outside the box. I know that nothing in life is absolute. My creative thinking can sometimes yield better results than conventional ideas. I allow myself to divert from the norm and consider alternatives that may even be unpopular until I show that they will work. I believe that I can convert a negative outcome into a positive one by changing my approach.

I am open to listening to the views and suggestions of others, as their experience or ideas may provide the perfect solution to a current challenge.

Perspective Re-Posturing Exercise

Today, your mission is to always aim at success, regardless of the situation. If one approach fails to deliver your desired results, simply try again with a different approach.

Reflection Questions:

1. How do I feel if I am unable to come up with a suitable solution right away?

2. Do I empower my team at work to think outside the box?

3. Do I share my strengths in problem solving with others?

Perspective Posturing: I Learn From My Mistakes

I live life each day with the knowledge that I make errors. I fully accept there are times when I do things incorrectly. I might choose one thing when another is the better choice. Or I make an impromptu decision that may later prove to be less than the best option for me.

Even though I am less than perfect, I learn from my mistakes in order to live the good life I deserve. I approach my mistakes and the mistakes of others with an open mind and heart.

When I figure out the errors of my ways, I evaluate how I made each mistake and then examine the consequences of those decisions. I ask myself, "What new knowledge do I have from this error? How can I use this knowledge now?"

I know the most important aspect of my evaluation is figuring out what I can learn. Realizing the lessons from my errors is a rewarding part of my day.

Perspective Re-Posturing Exercise

Today, if you make a mistake, you can diligently acknowledge the wrongdoing, evaluate the situation, and extract new knowledge from it. Your life will be enriched whenever you glean new information from your mistakes.

Reflection Questions:

1. Do I make it a point to learn something from my mistakes?

2. What are some valuable lessons I have learned from past errors in my life?

3. How can I keep my mind open to accepting my mistakes and learning from them?

Perspective Posturing: I Embrace Opportunities

I love the fact that life throws out many opportunities to me. No two days are the same because of the unique chances I get to do something positive in my life. I embrace these opportunities that give me a chance to change things for the better.

I am very open to new experiences in the workplace. When an opportunity comes up for transfer to a new department or to be a part of a new project, I jump at it right away. At work and home, I enjoy partaking in new activities that can broaden my horizons.

Learning is the key to development and you can only learn if you allow yourself to be open to change. I even like the idea of moving to a different part of the world because I get the chance to learn about new cultures. This prospect allows me to be more open to the views of others and accepting of differences.

I look for the kind of break that results in me being a happier and more successful person. I consider such opportunities as revelations from the Creator that it is time for me to move on to something else in my life.

Perspective Re-Posturing Exercises

Today, embrace changes that can create goodness in your life. Know that your family and friends only want the best for you and will support you in these endeavours.

Self-Reflection Questions:

1. Do I discuss new opportunities with my loved ones before going after them?

2. Have I shared my positive experiences with others I care about?

3. How do I determine if a new opportunity can bring positive changes to my life?

Perspective Posturing: I Follow Through On My Decisions

Even though I appreciate how smooth my life is, I also recognize my part in designing it. I recognize that one major aspect in life is facing the challenge of making decisions. I view decision-making as the weighing and measuring of different options.

I thoroughly explore my choices in any given situation. I ponder the how and why of an option. I imagine how a particular option can affect my life. I select the best choice based on my interpretation of each of the choices.

Once I reach the point where I make the decision, I am able to move swiftly ahead. I trust the effort I put into the decision-making process. When it comes to living out my choice, I eagerly move forward. It makes me proud to know that I waste no time in putting my decisions into play.

Although I sometimes make an error, it's okay with me because I know that making my best decision might still lead me down a challenging path. I know deep inside that I select the options that best meet my needs and wishes.

Perspective Re-Posturing Exercise

Today, be confident that your decision-making process compels you to choose the best option for the most positive results. Then you can follow through without hesitating.

Reflection Questions:

1. How do I perform when it comes to following through on my decisions?

2. In which situations do I hesitate in putting my choices into play?

3. Are there changes I can make in how I employ decision-making to encourage better follow-through with my decisions?

Perspective Posturing: I Deserve To Be Happy And Successful

Everyone deserves to be happy and successful, including me. Happiness and success are things that I create in my life. I purposely take certain actions that facilitate my happiness and success. I focus on the good things that life has to offer rather than spending my energy bemoaning my challenges.

I am a good person. I do many fine things. I am kind, generous, and work hard. All these things contribute to the joy and fulfilment in my life.

I deserve to experience great happiness on a daily basis. I am certainly worthy of it. I remind myself of all my blessings on a regular basis and find it easier to experience happiness.

Even if happiness and success try to elude me, I can catch them. I have all the ability I need. I have all the talent I require. Success and happiness are mine.

I can see success over and over in my life. I use my past successes to provide confidence now. Success and excellence are a part of who I am.

Perspective Re-Posturing Exercise

Today, take positive steps to ensure your happiness and success. Spend time doing things you love to do. Surround yourself with loving people. Renew your commitment to your goals. You deserve to be happy and successful.

Reflection Questions:

1. *How happy and successful am I right now?*

2. *What are some things I can do to improve my levels of happiness and success?*

3. *Why do I deserve to be happy and successful?*

Developing Spiritual Resources

Daily meditation helps clear my mind of those beliefs and habits that are getting in the way of me doing the work I was sent to do. Going for walks in nature, and reminding myself of my "why" statements, are also techniques I use to help remind myself that this journey is bigger than my own desires. This is about a calling to serve people, to fulfil my calling, to apprehend purpose, to fulfil the function for which I was created, and to honour those who have gone before me by the way I live my life.

Forming Emotional Resources

Surround yourself with likeminded people. You cannot do this alone. Thinking that you do not need anyone's help is not a good idea when taking such a courageous journey.

Reaching out to the other escapees is the beginning of forming my escape team. They are a huge part of my story, and each championed the book in a different way. This book itself is another part of developing my emotional resources.

This book is my 'homing beacon', calling out those who are also ready to escape and encouraging them to break free with me. I will talk later about how to form your own escape team and what questions I learned to ask as I put my own together.

Building Physical Resources

Getting and staying healthy not only increases energy and happiness, it allows you to experience newfound pleasure in pursuing your dreams and passions.

Taking care of my body, as you know from having read previous chapters, is an area of struggle for me. However, that doesn't mean it isn't important. I know that it is. If anything, my story provides a cautionary tale about what happens when you neglect this area of your life.

Right now, I am focusing on practicing self-care daily by eating healthy meals and staying hydrated. I will be the first to admit that I am the kind of person who tends to work into the early hours of the morning, trying to cram as much into my life as possible. I still do not get all the sleep that I need each night, but I am putting plans together that will allow me to make that change. I am beginning to understand that I can't do my best work when my body isn't getting what it needs to support the work of my brain.

Securing My Financial Resources

If you're like me, the hardest part of making the escape is securing the financial resources to cover your current living expenses and the amount over and above that which you would need in order to create the lifestyle you would like to be living.

Begin by deciding how much, per month, you would need to be bringing in to feel comfortable leaving your 9 to 5. How many monthly students would you need in your program in order to be able to leave, assuming they pay full price? How many would you need if they were to pay in installments?

How many months would you need to be able to go without that income in order to build your clientele and establish your reputation? Take the monthly amount you would need to be secure and multiply it by the number of months you would need before you could reasonably expect to begin making that income on a regular basis in order to determine your financial resource needs.

To get your financial resources together, you would then walk yourself through the following questions:

What Are My Monthly Expenses?

Knowing what is spent and where it goes is an important part of planning. Place a star beside those expenses that are non-negotiable. Things like rent, utilities, phone service.

Which Expenses Can Be Eliminated?

Can you eat out less? If you work from home, will you still need to pay for a daily commute? If you are currently paying for childcare, will you still need to pay for that? Any expenses that can be eliminated, even if it on a temporary basis, frees up financial resources to pursue your dreams.

Which Expenses Can Be Reduced

Sometimes expenses can be reduced by, for example, moving to a less expensive home or taking the money used on a monthly lease and instead buying a less expensive version of the same item. These little savings can add up quickly.

What Do I Need That I Can Trade to Get?

Not everything that might be on your list of things you need for your business must be paid for in cash. You might be able to work out a trade deal, exchanging services to get the help or space I need.

What Do I Have That Can Be Sold?

Aside from the program you are creating, what other items do I own that I might be able to sell in order to raise the cash you need? Can you hold a garage sale or rummage sale?

What Savings or Retirement Could I Tap Into?

A savings or retirement plan can be used to help you launch your business. It's a risk, but it can be worth the risk to gain the reward.

Would Someone Be Willing to Invest in Me?

Working for an investment management firm, I know that there are people out there who are willing to take risks in order to reap financial rewards later. Can you get some of the people you know to invest in your vision and help you make it a reality? What could I offer as a return on their investment?

Could I Crowdfund for the Money?

Crowdfunding is a popular option. There is as much art to it as science, but it can work and work well. You would need to investigate your options and put a plan into place that would include incentives that people would be excited to receive, but this is a viable possibility.

Could I Partner With Someone Else?

A partnership might be one way to start your business. That partner might bring the finances and connections you need to get started quickly. You also might consider partnering with someone who has a business already begun but is overwhelmed trying to serve all their existing clients.

DO YOU, BE YOU

When things fall apart
When the world's no longer at ease,
The rich also cry,
The bold and beautiful too!
But all said and done
When the old cock crows at dawn
The determined always win.
So do your thing, be true to you
Sing your song, in your own voice
Keep the faith, ignore the noise
Problems do not come to stay
When with fear you've fought and won
With great poise you can stand and say,
Yes, I did it my own way!

Clara Rufai

Chapter 7:
Developing Resilience

Resilience is the capacity to recover from difficulties and adapt to circumstances as they arise. Getting this book from start to finish in time for my launch date is testing every ounce of my resilience and has been an excellent exercise in developing it for the day when I am ready to finally make good my escape.

Nothing Goes as Planned

My plan for my book was simple: write the book, publish the book. I did not realize everything it would take to get from the writing of it to the publication of it. I knew that it would take some time to get the interviews completed and returned to me. I knew that it would take some time to get a cover designed and readied. Beyond that, I did not have enough experience to know what to expect.

Deadline after deadline was missed. I was continually challenged to revisit and revise my plan of attack. New information continued to surface and details that I was not even aware needed to be looked at were brought to my attention. My resolve to have my story put out and to meet my deadline was put to every imaginable test.

I share this with you because my experience is an excellent example of why you need to develop resilience. No matter how good your plan, there will always be things that come up along the way that you were not expecting. You will need to become good at adapting and forming new strategies to meet the challenges you face.

Editing Proves Challenging

Despite hiring two editors, and editing the manuscript myself, we still ran into major issues with the manuscript when it was put into the hands of test readers. There were inconsistencies brought to light with their help that needed to be resolved quickly and decisively. I am required to make tweaks to ensure that the promises made on the back of the book are delivered within the content of the book.

Remember that in an earlier chapter I told you nothing is ever going to be perfect? This book proves the case. It is not perfect. It is as perfect as I have been able to make it. However, if I held back the content waiting for that perfect day, when every single word in it met with everyone's approval, I promise you it would never have seen the light of day.

Incidentally, if you do find errors, I encourage you to send them to me at clara@clararufai.com. They may well provide occasion and reason for writing another book.

The Truth about Independent Publishing

When I chose to go the route of independent publishing with my book, I did not realize just how involved the process would be. There are a myriad of details to be put into place. Each of those details contributes to the final look and feel of the book and to the professionalism of it. It also makes a huge difference in how well it sells when it finally is released.

As an independent publisher, it isn't just the book I'm responsible for preparing. It is also the launch. I discovered I must be in charge of my own publicity campaign. I must recruit the people who will help me promote the book to others. I must make the decisions about pricing, covers, formatting, distribution channels, ISBN numbers, and bar codes. Every detail is my responsibility as the publisher. With an already full plate before me, this was no mean feat, and there were many times when it felt like it'd be far easier to just give up.

I am encouraged by just how much putting this book together and working through the steps of getting it ready to launch have prepared and are preparing me for life on the outside.

As those who have escaped can tell you, the same things that are true about independent publishing are equally true about being in business for yourself. You wear many different hats. You are the accounting team, the marketing team, the sales team, and the promotions and public relations team. The buck stops with you. Everything is your responsibility.

Even when you hire outside help, the final results are still ultimately your responsibility. It is your job to make sure your workers stay on task and are clear on what you want them to do. It is your job to be sure that the work they do is up to your specifications. It is your job to be sure that they represent you in the manner you want to be represented. Your reward for your hard work is that you get to keep the profits and take the credit at the end of the day.

What It Takes to Be a Best Seller

It is an eye-opener when you learn what goes into making a book a best seller. If you want to wind up on the New York Times Best Sellers List, you must sell 9,000 copies in a single week and those purchases must come from numerous sources. Imagine getting the entire town of, say Queensferry, to purchase your book in one week. It's a sizable feat.

To become a best seller on Amazon requires a third of those sales. It's still a challenging number, one that can seem daunting. You will need all the help you can get to reach the numbers. There are services that will guarantee you a spot, but the fees for such services begin at $20,000 and the costs can go upward into the hundreds of thousands of dollars.

In a recent Forbes Magazine article, a speaker by the name of Soren Kaplan achieved the 3,000 copies sold mark by getting his corporate clients to agree to purchase copies of his book as part of his speaking fees, along with purchasing copies for resell. It's a tactic that has caught my eye.

Scrambling for Proof Copies

Just when I thought I gave myself plenty of time to get proof copies ready and ordered, I was offered the opportunity to appear on Television. I did not have time to go the route I'd planned and get the books in hand. I was forced to think on my feet and search for an alternative production source, one that operated. That source needed to be based in London so that I wouldn't have to worry about shipping or customs delays. I was fortunate enough to find one.

The books arrived just in the nick of time, and I was saved the embarrassment of showing up without tangible evidence of my work in hand. Again, this was a test of my resilience. Could I adapt when things moved more quickly than I expected or planned for? I am happy to confirm that I could, and I did.

In life and business, as in books, opportunities may come before you feel fully ready to take advantage of them. These opportunities may not show upcome again. You must do what you can to capitalize on the situation, even if it means making sacrifices to do so. I would have preferred to wait until my manuscript was polished before printing the proof, but waiting would have meant missing the chance opportunity to gain the publicity that might help my book become a best seller.

The Value of Testing Your Product

Although testing the book with readers did mean additional work to be done, and although it presented additional challenges, it was invaluable. I can only imagine what the reviews might have been had we put it out there as it was. As it is, I am confident the product does exactly what is promised and delivers the strategies needed to help those who dream of breaking free of their prison. It offers them a path forward in making it a reality.

Doubt in your product, service, or your personal brand can prove detrimental to your business. The only way to pre-empt and cure doubt is to secure ensure that what you have produced does what you promised it will do. The only way to check and ensure this is to allow a small group (an advance party of people) to test it. Only then will you know where the problems are and what needs to be corrected, polished or tweaked to make your work be the best it can be.

Allowing your work to be tested before release is an act of responsibility. It is part of living up to your Shine Factor. Shining means that you always aim to offer your best work and produce the best material you possibly can. You do not fall into the folly of allow yourself to release shoddy work. You strive for excellence in everything you do as opposed to settling for sloppiness and nonchalance.

"Taking the path of least resistance only leads us to a place where we cannot have the utmost respect for, and faith in, our ability to persevere and to overcome" – Clara Rufai

---

Reworking the Plan Until the Plan Until It Shines

My original plan for the book didn't work 100%. It didn't deliver all of the content I wanted to offer my readers. It wasn't explicit enough in carrying my message. Thanks to my esteemed beta readers for investing the time to review the book for me, under tight timelines. Their feedback suggested additional work was required. I decided a mini overhaul was needed.

I went back to my editors and we spent an entire evening reworking the plan so that we could be sure everything that was promised would be delivered to the reader. The manuscript was dismantled, rearranged, and rewritten to match the new plan. It was painstaking and tedious work, but the result was a much better book, a much more thorough coverage, and a foundation to begin building my dreams.

As it was with my book, so it is in business. If the original plan you create does not hold up to testing, rework it until it does, even if that means you must completely dismantle and strip it to the core. You may have to toss out some parts and create new bits to fill in gaps, but what you will come up with is a much better version of what you had when you started.

This is a good place to introduce to you the queen of resilience herself, Joanna Oliver. Her consulting business, 'ConsultaChameleon' is based around the concept of resilience and flexibility. She does not let anything stop her.

Meet Joanna Oliver

Joanna's is a coach, mentor, counselor, trainer, public speaker, writer, and video producer through her business 'ConsultAChameleon.' In addition, she is also a published academic author and has developed learning programmes in personal development (Grow Free From Shackles), speaking (The Ultimate Guide to becoming a super-skilled speaker, trainer or lecturer) - which is also a book, Identity Development in children and young people (The Confident Chameleon) and concepts for professional growth 'working with what's in your hands - www.inyourhands) and 'heart-flow business growth.

Joanna is currently writing a book '52 ways to Grow Your Colours' and also contributing a chapter to a book about women of colour in academia.

She works part time in strategic development and copy writing for a fostering agency, is a Senior University Lecturer, a mum of three wonderful children - a teenager, a pre-teen and a toddler. They currently live in Kent – the garden of England.

She has a diverse background, having left school at fifteen years old and has been employed in a range of jobs over the years. She grew up in the Midlands and made her way to London in the 90's, via Bournemouth, where she obtained her first degree in Advertising, Media and Marketing. She went on to complete her Masters in Therapeutic Child Care in 1998, completing her dissertation the night before she gave birth to her first child. She has qualifications in:

- Professional supervision
- FE Teaching
- NVQ Assessing
- Youth Work
- Coaching

She offers many years of experience in teaching, training and undertaking therapeutic and functional group work with others. Joanna has spoken in a range of European countries, at Academic conferences, including Milan, Padua, Thessaloniki and Seville and has undertaken doctoral research in collaborative working. She has many skills, gifts and experiences in her hands to work with and these all contribute to her varied personal and professional colours.

She has rarely been in a 9-5, although prior to having her third child, she worked full time at the fostering agency. It was definitely a process. She started there as a consultant, then worked part time, and over the course of about six years, increased her hours to full time, which lasted until she went on maternity leave in June 2014.

The company always wanted her full time but she was always reluctant. She has enjoyed such a colourful career so far, but it wasn't easy to make the commitment to one role. If the company hadn't been so receptive of her entrepreneurial style, she would have moved to full time hours.

She struggled with being defined by a role or job description and the limitations that these place upon creativity and autonomy. She also struggled with having to feel 'beholden' to one workplace and the notion of static office working does not bring out the best in her. In order to go full time, she had to give up her employed work at a University but at that point, she was feeling tired and needed to 'settle' somewhere, so being full time at one place was attractive.

Planning the Escape

She found that it was better for her to transition by first, researching, imagining, visualising (including vision boards) and to then just let the compulsion for change overwhelm her to the point where change was inevitable. It constitutes 'inspired action' for her. In the past, she had to consider her role as main breadwinner and mum and made many career decisions based upon finance.

However, over recent years, especially since the birth of her third child in June 2014, she shifted her focus to quality of life. If she were to overthink implications, she would remain stuck but she currently has a very clear list of priorities for her life and financial wealth is lower down - after health, children, and passion (in that order).

She also leans much more into God for guidance. This takes her focus away from the material, to one of contentment 'whatever' and knowing that God will always provide, as long as she follows His guidance and hears Him correct her when she is going off course.

Life after the Escape

Joanna is a free spirit and likes to control her own time. As she grows older, this part of her has become more prevalent. She likes to free flow and go with her vibe, which is hard to do in the rat race. The rat race has little scope for evolving and morphing, which is something that is part of her professional identity.

She loathes having to be somewhere between certain times because someone else is telling her to. Although money justifies this for a little while, it does not offer enough compensation for her to suppress her true calling, which is priceless.

It sounds cliché to say she needs to live life on her terms but that is the reason. The work/life/money scenario is man-made and does not play to our sacred gifts. Joanna believes we could live sustainably by sharing our gifts - bartering, as it were. Life is so short and we spend so much time working...it's a travesty really.

Joanna wants to grow something that reflects her and serves others, utilises her gifts with what's in her hands. She wants to build a culture around core values she believes in and can fully commit to. She does not have to abide by red tape and imposed bureaucracy – the list goes on. She has lots of ideas and her own business is just that...so she can let them loose.

Through her coaching, mentoring, training, writing, therapeutic intervention, Joanna wants to continue to utilise her voice and encourage others to do the same in whatever way suits their gifts and aspirations. She enjoys helping people to work with what is in their hands and nurture their sacred gifts. This is the basis for her business.

She wants to serve people who are seeking...men, women...people who know there is more and need encouragement to make more from what they already have. She will stay true to her ethos and mission and make her 'service' central. Joanna believes that as her gifts are ordained, there will always be a need for them.

She believes that everyone exists for a purpose, with a reason, and a mission to fulfil. Joanna intends to ensure that she expresses this and extends herself to others in this lifetime. There are many people struggling, seeking, suffering, lost, dissatisfied, or just want to be more of who they are...knowing she can help with this is amazing and she has to fulfil that purpose.

Sometimes people need to be able to share their innermost feelings, explore their limiting beliefs, explore their vision and be accountable to someone else. Her business helps people to build a bridge between here and there, then and now...and then again. It can be a 'behind the scenes' type of service and yet it is significant and life changing.

Joanna's Lessons on the Run

The main thing that she learned is that no situation that one is anxious or worried about is ever as difficult in reality, as it can feel in the mind's eye. Joanna learned to speak to her supporters, not the naysayers, when she was and is on the cusp of change, as they will reinforce positive development.

Not everything goes according to plan so researching, imagining and visualising are great as are mind maps, goal maps and vision boards, etc. These are useful ways of keeping the vision alive but the details are not often predictable.

Her resilience and flexibility ensure that she can adapt to changes that need to be made in order to acclimatise to new lifestyles. It is important to trust the process, as the reason why sometimes cannot be seen except in retrospect. She believes this goes hand in hand with having faith in God, who always knows the reason why and how.

It is important to act upon any desire for change. This desire may be an 'inkling' - but it is also a sign. It is important to nurture this inkling into being. The best ways to do this are:

- Begin breathing life into ideas - Feed them. Get clear about what the idea can look like in reality...its mission, it's aims, it's value, who it serves, etc. The more an idea becomes a tangible project, the harder it is to ignore.

- Consider ways to restructure use of time in order to give some energy to the idea. It sounds cliché to say that TV time can be time spent on the project BUT it's true. In fact, she has found that TV has been pushed right down on her list, purely because the project became more entertaining.

- Start planning an exit route. Is it possible to reduce hours? Will your employers agree to any flexibility? She wasn't planning an exit route when she reduced her hours but the bigger (ordained) picture wasn't clear to her initially...in hindsight, she can see that this was a crucial step in her exiting process.

Connect with Joanna

Facebook:
https://www.facebook.com/joannaforeverlivingcolours/
Email: joanna@consultachameleon.co.uk

The Nail-Biting Wait

Literally days from the final deadline to order the books for my launch, the finished manuscript was returned to me. Those days when I waited for the work to be done were painful. The anxiety was real. There were so many variables, so many chances that things could go wrong. And so little time to fix things if they did.

The wait was worth it. The new version of my book came out much better. Some of what I'd written did not make it in the final version, but would be saved for use in other endeavours. There was no doubt in my mind, however, that I made the right call in working with beta readers.

When life's deadlines loom and you find yourself with nothing to do but wait, this is a very good time to focus on self-care, to meditate, to catch up on sleep and other things you may have been neglecting during the crunch time. You need to be at your very best when the big moment arrives to finally escape and to reveal your shine.

We should strive for improvement in whatever we do.

We should take ample opportunities throughout the day to improve our game and congratulate ourselves.

We should try hard to do better than yesterday.

Clara Rufai

Chapter 8:
Assembling My Escape Team

Part of any effective transition plan includes building a team, a solid group of individuals that you can rely on to help you break free and keep you accountable for taking action toward relocating into freedom. I am still in the process of assembling my transition team, and I invite you to be part of that team.

While I work to build my team, I am releasing this book as a homing beacon to other like-minded individuals who are feeling similarly trapped by their 9 to 5 position. This is a call to those who agree there has to be more to life than a 9 to 5.

I share with you the stories of those who have made their escape so that you know what to expect. But here is the reality: every escape will be different because the layout of every prison is different. To be effective, you must take full accounting of your own circumstances.

What Is an Escape Team?

An escape team is a group of like-minded individuals who are focused on achieving the same goals and are willing to support you in yours. Developing these relationships and interacting with other people who understand not just where you are headed but also what you are going through will enrich your life while you are waiting the day of escape. These relationships provide the recognition, support, love, and invaluable feedback you need to support you in your journey to freedom.

I am personally a member of several different groups of women who are aspiring coaches or corporate professionals seeking an entrepreneurial lifestyle. The connections with these women reminds me that I am not alone and encourages me when I am struggling.

I invite you to join my Shine Academy Facebook group so you can get the help and support you need as you work to find your Shine Factor and relocate to your Shine Zone.

Why Does It Matter?

You have a Shine Zone. When you work outside your Shine Zone, you get diminishing returns; the strife is real and the stress piles up. You are also a finite being with a limited amount of time and knowledge available to you. You need other people to be strong where you are weak and to help you get more done than you can on your own.

You can start a business, write a book, or do virtually anything on your own – but it will never be as good as it could be, as successful as it could be, without help. The more help and support you have, the more likely you are to succeed. This is mainly because that translates to more people watching out for you, alerting you to danger, and helping you to strategize when things don't go according to plan.

Another thing having an escape team does for you is to hold you accountable for results. Your escape team is in on this. They have a vested interest in seeing you succeed. It means their success, too. And if you let them down, if you fail to deliver, they are going to let you know about it. Not because they want to be mean, but because they are depending on you. That accountability leads you to think and act differently than you would if it were only yourself you were letting down.

Picking Your Team Mentor

The first team member that you should pick is your coach. Seeking out a professional, such as a life coach or someone in your ideal profession, provides an excellent, non-judgemental environment for building your "shine factor." You will be able to get in touch with your emotions and build your self-awareness.

Professional support will also help you eliminate any negative thoughts or negative behaviours that might get in the way. You can also receive guidance when it comes to achieving the more challenging areas of your plan of action. You may need help - do not hesitate to ask for it.

The mentoring of a coach is invaluable. They know where the dangers and pitfalls are, they know the challenges you'll face once you're outside the prison gates, and they know what you'll need to do in order to make good your escape.

Assessing Potential Team Members

Joining groups and getting involved in organizations is a great way to meet new people and begin scouting for the other members of your team. If you're joining a Facebook group, be on the lookout for people who actively post and evaluate their posting. Is this someone whose skills you could use? Do their values, personality, and goals align with yours? Do they offer something to the team that you need and do you offer something that they need?

Also look at their attitude towards others. Do they treat others with respect? Do they express gratitude? Are they someone you could see yourself working with in a crisis or when you are "in the trenches"? If you can't honestly answer yes to those questions, it doesn't matter how skilled they are or how many connections they offer. They aren't likely to add value to your team.

Listen to what others have to say about them, both the positive and the negative. This can tell you something about their character, too. Of course, you should not base your final decision on the words of others or on idle gossip, but it should be taken into consideration before making an invitation.

Inviting Potential Team Members

Making an approach is a moment of anxiety for many people. It doesn't have to be. Simply explain what you've observed about them, why you would like for them to be on your team, and what you feel you have to offer that would benefit them. Then let them make the next move.

Be the best you can be. Put out your positive energy and assume that this person will like what you are doing and want to join you. Remember that your purpose in life is greater than you could ever imagine, and you will find a way to relocate into your Shine Zone whether this person joins you or not.

Not everyone is ready to escape, and for some perhaps not when you are. Not everyone is ready to leave behind their comfort zone and step out into the unknown. When you invite potential team members and you are rejected, don't look at it as a sign that you aren't liked. Look at it as a sign that this person isn't ready to escape.

Be Excited When Your Team Mates Succeed

Don't let a team mate's success in breaking free damage your relationship. Seeing a business associate, good friend or loved one succeed should bring tremendous feelings of joy and pride. The good that comes to them will affect you in a positive way, too.

Don't compare yourself to them. Comparing yourself to your peers may seem tempting but is not a good idea. Everyone is on their own journey of what they are manifesting or cultivating in their own life. Focus on what you want and desire. Pay attention to what you want and it will happen the way it is supposed to for you. Instead, look for what you have that might complement and add value to what they have.

Communicating with Your Team

Your team needs to hear from you. They need to be included in the planning of your escape agenda. They need to know where you are headed and what your plans are when you get there. They need to be kept informed when changes are made to the plan. The more information you give your team, the more they can support you in achieving your goals.

Share your escape agenda with them and let them give you their honest feedback about it. They may know things that will help them identify areas you have overlooked. They may ask questions that you haven't thought of. If you get a response from them that upsets you, ask them why they feel or think that way. You will benefit from the answers you get.

Working with the team members I put together for this book was invaluable. Their insights and suggestions were not things I would have thought of on my own. If I hadn't shared my plans with them, they could not have provided the help I truly needed and I would not have been able to benefit from their advice and insights.

Create Win-Wins for Everyone on the Team

Everyone on your escape team should feel they have benefitted from working with you to help you escape. They should be able to see progress on their own escape agendas. They should walk away feeling more hopeful and positive than they did before they met you.

When you teach others to 'pay it forward,' and set the example, you can make changes in the lives of the people that you reach every single day. When you are being your best self in your shine zone, and your focus is toward the highest good, you will get stronger. Your actions can make the world a better place. Trust that your actions will pay it forward and have a positive effect on many people.

As with everything I do, I want this book to be a game changer. I don't want it to be just another book gathering dust on your desktop or on your bookshelf. Out there, there's a community of people who need to connect with the central message, or with the many little messages, contained in this book.

I have a mandate to help you journey from the prison to your palace, even as I embark on that journey myself. This book is only the beginning of my expression of that mandate.

Someone who knows a lot about the importance of assembling an escape team is my friend, DJ Sobanjo, the only man I interviewed for this book. He specializes in helping coaches become profitable, and his success was made possible in part because of the escape team he found.

Meet DJ Sobanjo

DJ runs a company called Profit from Coaching. It is a company focused on helping coaches, speakers, trainers, and consultants build a profitable business around their passion for helping others. While this is his full-time career right now, it was not always so.

DJ always knew that he would be working in the people development space, but it would take a lot of twists and turns before that vision became a reality. After relocating to the U.K. at the end of 2000, he took a job as a station assistant at the London Underground to make enough money to bring his wife overseas. He was making less than twenty thousand pounds a year. His intention was to stay no longer than five years. That soon turned to more than ten.

During training and orientation, he saw those trainers doing exactly what he wanted to be doing. It gave him something to aspire toward. After leaving training and moving into working with operations, he saw that while there was a natural and expected path of promotion, he didn't feel called to follow that path. He saw it as something of a trap for most people.

He found a path that aligned with his purpose very early on in his employment. He initially started down the natural path but he'd already determined he didn't want to pursue that avenue because he knew it wouldn't take him where he wanted to go.

He faced many challenges in making the transition from operations to corporate. People would tell him he was the wrong skin colour for the job or that people from his line of work weren't usually chosen for corporate positions. He refused to believe any of that nonsense. His decision to reject their negativity was the first challenge in transitioning from the natural career path set in place for him.

It was very, very tough. He attempted to apply multiple times for positions in corporate but was consistently rejected. Rather than choose to cower down, feel miserable, and play the victim – which would have been easier to do – he chose not to allow it to kill his fire.

However, he chose to go back and learn what he could have done better so that he could work on that. He kept focusing on improving himself. He would read personal development books and invest in himself in his free time. Eventually, he was hired for his very first role moving away from working in operations to working in corporate management development.

It was such a large jump that his co-workers speculated that his boss probably knew him and favoured him. They didn't think he deserved it because they didn't know his story. They didn't know that he was doing a lot of work outside of work to get himself ready for where he wanted to go.

He heard their excuses. Many of those who were passed over for that role worked in corporate. But what they didn't realize was that his off time was not spent idle. They were spent in pursuit of his dreams. He was teaching, training, and building a business on the side while they were living their normal lives.

He treated his part-time business like it was a full-time operation and was coaching a number of people, so by the time he showed up for the interview, even though he was not a corporate guy and did not have a lot of corporate experience, he'd invested his time in developing the experience he needed to excel in the position.

That experience showed while he was being interviewed and assessed for the role. He thanks God that he did get it. He challenges anyone who is reading this to let their dreams be big enough that they will invest their five to nine to work on preparing themselves for when they're going to be invited to be in front of Pharaoh like Joseph was.

Moving from the London Underground to the corporate Transport for London was a dream come true. Management training confirmed that this was exactly what he wanted to be doing. He wanted to train leaders, to coach managers, and work with them to equip them for that path.

He spent the first three years of his new job mastering his new role, doing a lot of training in a wide variety of programs from front line management to middle management, senior management, and executive management teams. The dynamics of the various teams within the organization were so different that it really felt like he was a consultant working within different companies.

The work developed him as a consultant, coach, trainer, and he got really comfortable in his job. He felt truly privileged to be in the position that he was in because the boss he ended up working for was very entrepreneurial and became like a coach. She knew his aspirations and actually worked to help him prepare and plan for his eventual escape. She knew that helping him to achieve his goals and dreams would make him a more productive and satisfied employee, which it did.

Another person who mentored him was his pastor, who was a successful marketplace entrepreneur. He understood the process and the journey and was able to guide and mentor him. That support and encouragement was a critical component of his success and ability to stay positive through the inevitable challenges he faced along the way. His pastor was ready and willing to share his strength, capability, and expertise.

He felt he was being prepared and groomed for the future he desired. He was enjoying his job so much and the scope of his role was expanding so much that, for a while, he hesitated to leave. He got an opportunity to leave and go do something, but changed his mind and stayed back. He was too comfortable where he was.

Shortly after that, things began to change in his work environment. His boss was promoted elsewhere within the business and a colleague of his was promoted into her role. He was a great guy, but the dynamic was not the same. He stopped enjoying his job. He realized God was pushing him to take that step and leave behind his comfort zone by taking it away from him.

Planning the Escape

His company began to go through a restructuring and there was not a lot of communication happening. He felt they were doing a terrible job of helping the employees prepare for what was coming and he wanted out. He continued building his business on the side while looking for the right time to leave.

He referred a coaching program to his clients and got a few subscribers. The company he referred them to then paid him to work with them for a month. It was tiring work. He would come back home mentally exhausted from his 9 to 5 work to start coaching sessions. A month later, he became sick for a week.

During that week he realized that he could make some money doing this program, but not the way his life was right then. Combining his 9 to 5 work with his 5 to 9 work was unreasonable.

His 9 to 5 work was very intensive and he was sitting on the phone or on Skype, trying to have a consultation with someone, when his brain was too tired to think. That experience let him know that people were willing to pay him for his expertise. It was a confidence booster.

He knew what he needed to do to grow a business, so when he was offered the opportunity to leave in exchange for a small amount of money that would give him a year's financial buffer while he tried to navigate his path, he decided to take advantage of it.

Life After the Escape

Where the business is today has been a journey of pivoting until he finally found himself where he is. This is the same for many people who are starting out.

He started out helping small and medium sized business owners develop marketing systems and strategies to get them more clients, but never felt comfortable or confident in that space. He then began a training consultancy working with corporate clients.

At one point, he made in two weeks what some people made in a year. He took everything that came his way as long as it aligned with his passion for helping people. However, he wasn't treating his business as a business and so when the money stopped coming in at the end of 2012, he was faced with a shocking reality. He'd been in business for a long time. He'd learned marketing, selling, training, and coaching. But he'd never learned how to build a business.

2013 proved to be a very different year for him. Things got extremely tough. He was struggling and debts were piling up as he used his credit cards to keep things going. He was very, very close to throwing it all in and going back to a nine to five because he had a family that needed him. He would sit in front of his computer in the morning, see the pile of bills beside the table, and begin crying. He didn't know what to do.

A friend of his invited him to come and speak at one of his events. He took a course he'd created the previous year, put together a webinar to teach people how money is really made online, and sold the course at a discount at the end of the webinar if they paid right then. 100 people showed up for the webinar and 30 of them bought the online course for 200 pounds each. They made 6,000 pounds in one afternoon.

He was began thinking like a business owner. This was where things began turning around for him.

He stopped making passion decisions and began making business decisions that aligned with his passions. Having passions without the business decisions, he realized, was a lot like having fuel in a car but no particular destination in mind. He knew he needed to focus his passions on becoming profitable.

His time was a valuable commodity. When being asked to do work without getting paid, he would ask himself whether he could afford to give away the time for free. He would also ask himself what the business purpose of performing that charitable work was. If there was no business purpose, and he could not afford to give away his time as a donation to a charitable cause, he would politely refuse the offer.

By the end of 2013, though, after coming back from two or three months away from his family in Sierra Leone, he came back tired and exhausted. He knew he hadn't left his job to be away from home this much. He asked himself what it was he really wanted to do. He realized what he really wanted to do was be at home to be a father to his children, not travelling into London every day or going all over the world so that he was never home

During 2013, he'd worked with a lot of coaches who were really good at what they did and were able to make a big difference but didn't know how to make money and he decided to build a business helping them. That was the start of Profits from Coaching.

He knew he needed to prove to the coaches that his ideas could work so he started a career development coaching program called "Accelerate Your Career" and ran it for a year, generating a full-time income, while he fleshed out the ideas for Profits from Coaching.

DJ's Lessons on the Run

1. Treat your business as a business. Make business decisions that align with your passions rather than passion decisions.
2. Just because you know elements of how to create money doesn't mean you know how to build a business. Get help from someone who does.
3. There will be challenges at every stage of your business building. Those don't go away, they just change.

Moving Forward Into the Future

He now makes more in a month than a lot of people make in a year and he never would have been able to make that happen if he hadn't made the transition. His biggest challenge now is keeping up with business growth.

Right now, his business is working on putting together quite a number of things. First, is to add structure to his community that will help more people coming in at different stages of their coaching, speaking, training, and consulting business. Second, five years from now they want to help one thousand coaches build a full-time income around their passion of helping others. That's a long-term five-year mission.

His team is consistently looking at ways to put things in place to be able to help people in a bigger scale, those who are driven, and he wants to work with people who are driven by a passion of helping others, who want to coach or consult or speak and who want to train to write. He believes that being able to build a full time business, and a full time business is anything from two thousand up to ten thousand pounds per month, because full time means different things to different people, would help change the lives of so many people.

Contact DJ:

Website: http://www.profitfromcoaching.com/

Facebook:
https://www.facebook.com/groups/CoachesSpeakersAndAuthors/

S.M.I.L.E

Keep on smiling and one day life itself will get tired of upsetting you.

Never let the silly little things of life steal your happiness.

#BeingHappyNeverGoesOutOfStyle!

Stay Trapped In Happiness!

Clara Rufai

Chapter 9:
Creating Your Escape Agenda

With all the pieces put together, it is time to formulate your escape agenda. The escape agenda is part business plan, part launch plan, part visualization board, and part goal chart. It is there to help keep you motivated and moving in the direction of your dreams. It is your plan on how you will get from where you are to the life you want to be living.

What Is Included in an Effective Escape Agenda?

Focus on becoming your best self

It isn't a destination, it's a process

It's a journey - with ups and downs

Yet through it all, your eye must be keen

Your vision clear as day

Determination is the key.

An escape agenda should include the following:

1 - Your Shine Factor Statement

2 - Your Shine Factor Story (this should act as your basic biography for engaging press or when describing yourself to prospects.)

3 - Your Shine Factor Delivery Plan (this should include the offering you will be delivering)

4 - A plan for reaching out to the people who are most likely to need it

5 - It also includes a timeline for the escape,

6 - A checklist of the resources you'll need,

7 - Strategies for obtaining those resources along with timelines for obtaining them

8 - A list of your escape team members and their contact information

9 - Where you will relocate to and When

10 - A roadmap of how you will get to your Shine Zone.

Who Should Have Access to Your Agenda?

Obviously, your escape team and your escape mentor need to have access to that agenda. However, you might want to keep that agenda private until you are ready to break free from your prison. Employers might not be understanding if you are secretly planning a break out and might choose to hurry your exit before you are ready to leave.

If you have contractual obligations toward your employers, such as a non-compete clause or a clause which prohibits you from working for other employers at the same time as your present employer, you will need to take those obligations seriously. Failing to do so can result in a lawsuit, which could damage your reputation, and prohibit you from doing business.

Whether you share your agenda with family and friends is up to you. Some family may be supportive, some family may not. Keep your agenda handy, though, and review it regularly.

Visualizing Your Escape

The unknown can be frightening but replace that fear with a desire for your passion that you are following – visualize it each and every day. Picture yourself doing your passion, whatever that is. What does it feel like? What does it look like? Are there other people around you? Feel that energetic state of excitement that is your desire and you will be able to cultivate your passion more easily.

How does it feel to be living life on your terms? What do you spend your mornings doing? What opportunities have come your way because you decided to escape?

Create a vision board that shows you what it is you are working toward. For every vision you hold, give yourself a date by which you want to achieve those things. Visions without deadlines are not goals. They are wishes. Don't wish for things to change. Make them change.

Don't Just HOPE For It - STRATEGIZE For It

Don't Just PRAY For It - POSITION For It

Don't Just WAIT For It - ALIGN For It

Don't Just SEARCH For It - NETWORK For It

Don't Just WISH For It - PREPARE For It

Don't Just DESIRE It - COMMAND It

Don't Just BELIEVE It - EXPECT It

Don't Just OCCUPY - STRETCH & EXPAND

> *Don't Just PERFORM - IMPROVE*
>
> *Don't Just RE-THINK - RE-WRITE & RE-CREATE*

Create a Commitment Statement

As you move forward to your course of action, there are new habits and certain disciplines that will support your success in what you decide to do in your plan of action. You will need to consider how you will assimilate each of your new habits into your way of being as you execute your agenda.

It is not enough to simply have an idea of how you are going to do something; you must commit to exactly how you will make each of the necessary changes a habit in order to support your ability to stay the course throughout the entire process of becoming who you are meant to be.

Once you find your "shine factor," you must develop the habits that allow you to remain in the "shine zone". The process can be compared to bowling – even though at times your ball may go into the gutter, you probably still hit a few pins. Keep aiming for those pins that will keep you on your course of action.

Creating a commitment statement and signing it in front of your escape team is one way of getting yourself to take this commitment seriously. You want to make it as real as possible. More lives than just yours are counting on you.

Check and Monitor Your Progress

It is not enough to simply make an escape agenda. You must consistently follow it and monitor your progress against your original plan of action. Reflect on what is going right and where you are struggling. Are there areas in your plan that you are avoiding action?

Check and monitor your progress at the end of each month. Acknowledge what you have accomplished and identify new experiences or actions that will keep moving your forward into your "shine zone."

My personal shine zone is helping working women who feel unfulfilled and want to break away from the limitations of the 9 to 5 but are afraid and unsure of how to go about it to design a strategy that enables them to create an alternative income around their passions so that they can replace their 9 to 5 income while fulfilling their life's purpose.

My Shine Factor program is the first part of my system. Once I've helped them identify their Shine Factor, I'll help them relocate to their Shine Zone.

Strategies for Implementing the Agenda

As you learn how to improve and develop the real you, absorbing all of this information, you will need to put it to work for you. This book provides you with a step-by-step approach in finding your "shine factor."

You'll discover exactly what that is, through your actions and experiences, and how to break your emotion-driven behaviours and unconscious habits that may be getting in the way of achieving your full potential. This is necessary to break free from the 9 to 5 prison.

Each step is important and builds on the other steps. Do not skip through without completely understanding what you need to reflect on and all the exercises. Developing your shine factor can't be done without self-awareness and self-knowledge. That requires a great deal of introspection and reflection, which takes time.

You also can't find your shine factor without facing your fears, trying new things, and having experiences that change the neurological connections in your brain. Give yourself enough time to really understand and acknowledge each step in your game plan.

Talk About Your Success

Slow down and take time to talk about your successes with other people, especially other like-minded people. This will help you stay optimistic about your goal(s), build your self-esteem and confidence in yourself and your abilities. Get rid of that old belief that talking about your achievements is just 'tooting your own horn.' So what if it is - you have earned bragging rights.

Create A "Best Part of the Day" Activity

This will be different for everyone. For some, it may be your 'quiet' time in the morning perhaps in prayer or solitude. For others, it might be family time at the dinner table where you go around the table and everyone says what he or she enjoyed that day and why.

Use this time to share your "wins" or achievements that make you feel proud. Taking the time to do this one activity helps you get excited about what you are doing and stay focused. Share your experience and achievements with others.

Stand Firm In Your Beliefs

When you are a person of integrity, it will help keep you on an enriching and purposeful path in pursuing your goals. It can also help you maintain a positive outlook and make you feel happier inside, in general. When you stand firm in your behaviours and beliefs, the feedback and praise that you receive from others validates your actions and YOU in your "shine zone."

Dedicate Yourself to Development

It takes discipline, regular practice, and plenty of determination to change your brain over time. Think about all the practice it takes for those in sports, gymnastics or any new skill. We have to commit to the relationship skills, self-care, and development of our brain to make the changes needed to find our "shine zone."

Think about how long it took to learn how to swim or for a baby to walk. You must be prepared to dedicate yourself to own development in reaching your goal. Challenge yourself.

Celebrate The Clues Along the Way

Pursuing your passion or desire is like being on a treasure hunt. You may not have a clear path laid out in front of you but you get clues along the way that give you assurance that you are on the right path. Celebrate those clues. Use them as a reminder to not give up when your desired result is not happening as fast as you would like.

Focus On Mind Re-Mapping

I am investing my time in reading books that help me draw a brand new map of a life where I am in control of my own destiny and the power residing in me is given permission to soar, like the caged bird finally released. With each book I read, each resource I gather, and each networking opportunity I take advantage of, I am finding that my 'valid' reasons for staying fall away.

The mind is the birthplace of progress, purpose, and passion. It is also the well of negativity, indecision, and fear. As the late Myles Munroe put it, the 'the wealthiest place on earth is a cemetery.' He said this in recognition of the fact that far too many people go to their graves unfulfilled, because they never pursued or lived their dreams. I will not be included in those statistics.

I am finding a wealth of resources to dig into, sapping out wisdom and practical points as case studies. This is gradually but radically changing my perspective. Line upon line, precept upon precept, here a little and there a little, I am getting myself ready for the day when I can make my escape.

"The 9 to 5: if you don't belong, you'll find it difficult to stay; if you do belong, you'll find it difficult to leave. I knew I no longer belonged and had bigger dreams to pursue." – Clara Rufai

---

When Should You Time Your Escape?

There are signs when it is time for you to escape. These signs may come sooner than you expect. Pay attention to these clues and adjust your agenda accordingly.

Knowing the right time to move on is tough for many people. Changing your routine and dealing with the uncertainty of what comes next can be nerve-racking and stressful. Whether you realize it or not, you are moving into a time of greater inner peace and tranquillity.

Peace of mind means feeling secure, and knowing that you are always provided for. Even if your logical mind cannot possibly fathom how you are going to pursue your passion or how a challenge could be resolved, peace of mind means that you trust that God will create a miraculous solution for you.

Peace of mind is within you. You can feel peace, even in the midst of great turmoil or change. It is a mistake to think that you have to wait until your life is problem-free before you can be happy and peaceful. The opposite is true. Work toward serenity and then your life challenges will lessen and disappear. Serenity is your natural state of mind.

Health

With that said, the best way to figure out when the best time to make your move to your new passion or work on your dream is to look for the tell-tale signs that it is time to make a change. When your work begins to adversely affect your health, it is time to move on. Dissatisfaction with your working conditions, or type of work in general, can cause a variety of health problems that include:

- Depression
- Weight loss
- Weight gain
- Chronic fatigue
- Frequent illnesses
- Feeling of helplessness

- Anger over the little things
- Trouble getting out of bed

All of these should be taken seriously as they can adversely affect your health, life, and family. Is your current job or career really worth risking your health? Pay attention to your physical body.

Boredom

Boredom is a good indicator that you are not fulfilled or being challenged by your work. Many people reach a point in their careers when they are simply bored with their occupation and feel they can contribute more to the world. Being bored can cause a good employee to stop caring about their work and that can lead to a reprimand or termination when you are not ready to make your move.

In the meantime, you can try to be more involved with other aspects until you are ready. However, being bored is definitely a tell-tale sign that it is time to move on and pursue your dreams.

Dreading Your Work

When you dread getting up to go to work in the morning, it is time to get serious about pursuing your passion. While you might still get excited when Friday finally arrives, but it is not good when you spend the weekend dreading when Monday comes around. If find yourself feeling like this more often than not, it is time to move on and pursue your passion.

Interfering With Family

Any job can be demanding, but if you are in a profession that requires you to work endless long hours or you must be 'on call' any day of the week, it can certainly affect you as well as your family.

Some people thrive on this type of work schedule, but if you are trying to spend time with your family or want a 'date night' with your spouse, chances are you are not very happy with your situation. When a job interferes with your family, and life in general, it is definitely time to move on.

Finding Balance While You Are Working On Your Escape Agenda

This is a challenge for me, but it is important. It does not do you one ounce of good to plan an escape and work such long hours that you put yourself into the grave trying to dig yourself out of the prison.

It is also important not to forget that the people whom you care about need time and attention, too. They are the reason you are working so hard to escape. Don't neglect them to the point where they no longer feel wanted in your life.

As with any challenge you face, it's important to seek the help and support of someone who is experienced in dealing with it. One such woman I met and whose advice I value is Kathleen Zajac. She is a world authority in creating lives of harmony and balance for high achieving, successful women.

Meet Kathleen Zajac

A former accountant who is now an experienced energy healer, harmony mentor, and meditation teacher, Kathleen was once employed by the world's biggest investment banks. Working 9 tight deadlines per day, Kathleen experienced first handed stress, frustration, work overload and finally – burn out.

Instead of simply quitting her corporate job, she chose to stay, consciously face her life situation, and commit to inner work and self-development. Now she helps other high achieving successful women relieve stress and anxiety, take away pressure of time, work or family, create harmony and balance in their everyday lives, so they can finally fully enjoy each moment of their lives.

She began meditating at 13 years of age and eventually obtained an M.A in Sociology of Medicine, Health and Illness. Kathleen is extremely proud and honoured to be a founder and host of a thriving Facebook community of powerful women leaders called "Woman: Limitless, Powerful, Beautiful." This is a safe space co-created by amazing women, who are ready to explore the feminine side of leadership and create harmony in their lives.

Before becoming a life harmony mentor, meditation teacher and energy healer for high achieving, successful women, she was a highly driven goal achiever. She basically believed that whatever she desired – she would make it. Kathleen also believed that the harder the struggle – the more valuable a goal would be.

Filling Life with the Wrong Things

She intentionally created struggle in her life and studied two full-time Master Programmes at the university at the same time.

She secured each of her corporate jobs with a single interview. She worked full time as an accountant at one of the biggest investment banks in the world while doing full-time Ph.D studies in Sociology of Medicine, Health and Illness. Multiple tight deadlines was her normal.

Although most people are thrilled at the end of the day when something on their checklist can be crossed out, Kathleen was not. She would immediately create something else to add to her checklist. She didn't celebrate any of her successes because she was too busy reaching new, challenging goals.

At the same time, she was very dedicated to her spiritual growth. Her experiences with meditation at age thirteen led her to consciously working with energy and exploring various healing modalities. Her life was full and she thought,

"That's how things should be, that's how a happy, successful life looks like."

Her life was full of unhealthy, unbalanced relationships and energy-draining friendships. She was applying for the scholarships and internships to prove her worth.

Until one day when… she crashed. It all crashed.

It was a chilly Friday morning in early December in Dublin, when she woke up and couldn't move from her bed. She was so paralyzed by fear, tiredness, frustration and stress that her body rejected her. There was enormous pressure to close the fiscal year before the final deadline.

A Week of Reflection

She took a week off to fully commit herself to meditating, tapping into her subconscious, connecting with her soul and with God. That was the moment when, for the first time in her life, she honestly asked myself – "What do I want to create in my life now?" "How do I want my life to look like in 10 years' time?"

Spending the next 10 years at a corporate environment would have led her to more stress, higher blood pressure, migraines, and insomnia. Obviously, she did not want such a life for herself. She didn't want to pay such a high price for a safe life, with a payroll on her bank account every month.

While still working as a corporate accountant, she was able to reduce the level of stress, anxiety and fears on her own. She finally recognized the needs and desires of the part of her she had forgotten for years – the feminine part.

She worked a lot with the feminine energy (the divine feminine as many women call it), her creativity, capacity to receive (not only to give), and gave herself a lot of attention, love and tenderness. She restored a subtle harmony and balance in her life.

That week off was a real breakthrough moment for her. It was crystal clear to her she just opened a new chapter of her life. She left her corporate job 10 months later.

Planning the Escape

Transition was… painful to say the least. She was trying to apply the "corporate girl" mind set, as she called it, to the entrepreneurial world. She was doing everything she thought she should be doing and following each piece of advice she was given. It was creating more and more frustration for her. She was spending loads of money on unnecessary programs.

It took her over a year to free herself from that "corporate girl" mind set to stop making decisions based on "I should," I have to," "it sounds rational," "it makes sense," "it sounds logical" paradigm.

Switching into the new paradigm of thinking and living was challenging. As a woman entrepreneur, the number one skill she needed to master was to learn how to listen to her intuition. She had to learn to trust herself.

When employed, her personal responsibility was limited. She could enter a company and all she needed to do was to identify and follow the rules. When starting her own business, however, she needed to create everything from scratch.

It took her a while to finally trust herself, to recognize herself as the best decision maker in her business, to value and honour her voice. As a woman entrepreneur, she had to master "the feminine way" of doing business by creating, manifesting and using her imagination. It was a completely new world for her — a woman who was used to plans, procedures, time schedules, and rational thinking.

The second typical mistake most corporate women make when they enter the entrepreneurial world revolves around their working hours. When starting her business, she created another job for herself. She believed she needed to stay busy and do hundreds of things that can't wait. She was working 12 -16 hours per day. If she wasn't working, she felt guilty for not doing what she was supposed to do.

The truth is she was creating that entire 'struggle' to prove her worth. She simply didn't know the other way of doing things. She didn't know she could work 2 or 4 hours per day and still achieve the same, or even 10 times better, results in her business.

She said something to me that grabbed my attention.

"No, you don't have to work 10 or more hours per day to create your business. You need to work smart, not hard. We live in amazing times now, and for very little money, you can purchase systems that will automate a huge part of your business." – Kathleen Zajac

---

The transition stage made her cry more than a few times also because she felt very lonely. All her friends were working at corporations, and everyone in her family had 9 to 5 jobs. There was nobody, literally nobody, who could understand her fears, decisions she had to make, the worries, and her sleepless nights.

Her ex-partner was changing the topic each time she started talking about her business. He simply didn't treat it as a serious thing. For him, it was an irresponsible caprice of a bored little girl.

Life After the Escape

Kathleen could never understand the pressure created at the corporate environment – the pressure of the lack of time, of urgency of her work, goals which had to be achieved immediately. That schizophrenic gap between the real importance and value of her work and the artificial pressure created by management was growing steadily, until it reached the breaking point and she decided to quit.

She had already left her 9 to 5 corporate job. Now she only wishes she had asked someone to mentor her during the transition period, which was one of the most stressful and anxious times in her life.

In her case, it was a calling. She knew, in each cell of her body, that the path of being a woman entrepreneur was the right and only option for her. Her business is first and foremost about her, it helps her develop as a woman, as a human, as an entrepreneur.

Her business is a vehicle through which she can touch, inspire and transform the lives of hundreds of women. She works with professional women – either employed or entrepreneurs. They all have one thing in common – they hear the calling to become better, bigger versions of them. They understand the best investment they can ever make is to invest in their growth.

They are willing to invest their time, energy and financial resources to be supported and guided, so they can relieve their most hidden fears, worries, anxiety and eliminate the pressure of time, work, family or friends and create harmony in their lives on their own conditions.

She is forever grateful for having such an opportunity. She is creating the business that serves her. Thanks to her business and to the vibrant community she has created, she has touched lives and hearts of hundreds of women.

Watching her clients blossoming is a real privilege and she feels honoured and blessed to work with her amazing clients. They no longer live under constant pressure and no longer hold themselves back because of fear. They are able to free themselves from the pressure of other people's judgments, free themselves from old self-limiting beliefs, old pains and stories of failure. They discover a whole new paradigm or living and creating their life - the divine feminine way.

She believes in her message. She believes the leadership in the 21st century will awaken women, who are high achievers, who stand firmly in their power and unapologetically embrace their feminine side. It is high time we support every woman in becoming a successful leader in her life.

She is willing to support her clients in every way possible to help them become the most powerful, fearless and divine versions of themselves. By creating shifts, inspiring, teaching, guiding and changing the lives of her clients, she inspires and transform the lives of their partners, children, family, friends, and colleagues at work.

"We are all interconnected – it is the ripple effect. – Kathleen Zajac"

Kathleen's Lessons on the Run

For her, the only option was to move forward. Since starting her journey as a visionary woman entrepreneur, she never had a moment of doubt, even when she wasn't making any money in her business. The decision was made and she always had an unshakeable faith in her message. She created a vibrant community of gorgeous women, enrolled wonderful clients, shared her message, and finally felt fulfilled in her life.

Everything in her life serves her and works for her highest good. For many years it used to be the other way around. Yes, she still has challenging moments, fears both big and small, but she consciously chooses to face them. She learned to honour herself, to recognize and value her voice, and listen to her intuition. She learned there is no competition out there, only collaboration.

"Your message is unique, because your experience, wisdom, skills, knowledge are unique. Nobody can substitute for you. The power you have in your hands when you finally dare to live your life the way you desire, to make real that dream you have been postponing for years. It is hard to describe how great, breath taking and heart-touching this feeling is."

Kathleen feels extremely blessed to finally be fully in charge of her life. She feels blessed to be working with wonderful women, healing their past, releasing fears, worries and tensions and assisting them in making their secret dreams come true. What can be better than living the life from your dreams?

Choosing to be a visionary woman entrepreneur was the best decision in her life. She is forever grateful for having made her decision, despite all fears, doubts, and negative comments. At the end of the day, it is her life. It is your life.

More Tips

- **Connect and Surround Yourself** - with visionary women entrepreneurs who will understand your mission/secret dream, offer you a safety net of support and say, "Hey, that's a great idea! That's completely doable!"

- **Start Journaling** - write down your feelings, worries, thoughts, aha moments, and ideas. You will have evidence for yourself when your lower days come and your journal will show you how much you have already gone through and achieved. Plus you will start connecting with your intuition on a deeper level.

- **Recognize Your Life Is An Endless Beautiful Journey** - Each moment of now is absolutely precious, even if you feel stuck in your 9 to 5 job. Whatever decision you make now — it's ok. Don't beat yourself up with thoughts that you waste time or you are not good enough etc.

- **Consider Hiring A Mentor** - especially if your mind is full of self-limiting beliefs that sabotage your actions, such as "I am not good enough, I am not ready, who am I to do this?" etc. I would strongly advise hiring a woman (a mind-set coach, a divine feminine healer). Men operate in business in a different way, they create and manifest in a different way too, so you might end up feeling disappointed or frustrated by following the "masculine path". A mentor will help you raise your self-esteem, release fears or self-limiting beliefs, and uncover you true mission and dream

- **Be Honest With Yourself** - Give yourself permission to recognize and accept your deepest desires. No dream is too complicated, too high or too difficult. It is your dream. Own it. Only you have the power to make it real. Honour yourself and your desires.

Connect with Kathleeen

Website: http://kathleenzajac.com/

Twitter: https://twitter.com/kathleen_zajac

Facebook: https://www.facebook.com/zajac.kathleen

Advice for When You're Ready to Escape

Whether you finally decided to quit your job or were fired, it can be upsetting. There are some things you should avoid doing when that happens or when you make the decision to leave your job.

It can be an emotional time but do not tell your co-workers or boss what you really think of them. You may see them again down the road and perhaps may work with them again. They may become prospects or even future clients if handled right. You never know, so stop and think before saying anything you might regret later.

<u>Do Not Put Your Future in Jeopardy</u>

Never damage property or steal something from your place of employment. This is a criminal offense and never a good idea. In addition to the possibility of being put in jail, your professional reputation will be damaged by your actions.

<u>Ask for References Before You Leave</u>

Everything you accomplished at your workplace should be duly noted and used to your advantage in pursuing your dream or passion. It will allow you to share your talents and skills with those who need to know in your future. Do not give out anyone's name as a reference without permission. The person giving you a reference should know ahead of time that someone might contact him or her in the future.

You can ask for a reference by email because it will be easier for the person to decline by sending an email note instead of having to tell you in person.

Be professional and ask, "Do you think you know my work well enough to give me a reference?" or "Do you feel comfortable giving me a good reference?" This will give the person you ask a way out if he or she does not believe they could give you a strong endorsement or respond to someone who might call for a reference.

<u>Do NOT Speak Poorly of Your Employer, Co-Workers, or Place of Employment</u>

Your mother may have told you, "If you don't have anything nice to say about someone, do not say anything at all." Well, the same holds true for your workplace including your co-workers and/or boss. All it will do is cause undue stress on everyone involved. It could even result in a lawsuit.

The only person who will look bad is you. The thought may cross people's minds that you could have been at fault and you do not want any negative energy or attitude into your new world of passion. Furthermore, those you are attempting to persuade to work with you may wonder what you will be saying about them when all is said and done.

Chapter 10:
Your Shine Zone Relocation Package

The Shine Zone Relocation Package is designed to help you adjust to life on the outside by providing you all the tools you ·need to successfully make the transition into your new role by teaching you how to handle your new responsibilities and lifestyle.

Why Do I Need One?

Life on the outside is drastically different from life on the inside of a prison. You've been living in a corporate prison for most of your adult life. It is going to take some and some mental adjustment to get used to handling your newfound freedom. Up until now, other people have been making most of your decisions for you. They tell you what projects to work on, when to get them completed, and how to successfully complete them.

On the outside, you are going to be making those decisions for yourself. You're going to have to figure out which projects to work on and when. You're going to have to figure out how to successfully complete them and what results determine whether your work was successful or not. It's a learning process, and like any learning process there is a sharp learning curve to it.

Nothing but personal experience can get you completely ready for what is coming, but this chapter is designed to help. This chapter pulls from the experiences of the escapees you've met to give you an idea of what you'll need and what to expect.

What Do I Need in My Relocation Package?

Before you break out, you're going to need a new identity, a new role, the keys to your kingdom, assistance adjusting, and help avoiding recapture. It's one thing to find your Shine Factor. It's another thing to make the transition to living in your Shine Zone.

20% of the Relocation Package is systems and mechanics. 80% of it is mind-set work, personal development, and networking. That's because the hardest thing isn't actually doing business. It's keeping the business – and yourself – going when things don't seem to be working and you're facing discouragement and doubt.

I don't know any people who have gone into business for themselves and not faced discouragement and doubt. There are always struggles. Every level of success brings new levels of struggles with it. It is the struggles and the challenges that lead to the growth.

Adopting Your New Identity

At work, people may call me an Investment Management Professional, but that is not who I am. I am Clara I. Rufai, published author, and Headmistress of Shine Academy where I teach aspiring coaches, corporate professionals, and disadvantaged youth how to write, speak, and act so they can learn to express themselves, find the confidence to make their voice heard, and learn to present themselves in a way that inspires and entertains others.

I need to rehearse speaking my new identity as often as possible until it becomes so ingrained in me that it is a natural response when people ask me who I am or what I do. I also need to practice delivering the story behind my Shine Factor and how I discovered it so that I am prepared to talk about it when others ask me to tell them more.

Acting the Part

I need to get comfortable with what it means to be the Headmistress of Shine Academy. I must treat my new identity as if it were a role I am playing in a theatre production. How does a Headmistress of Shine Academy behave? How does she walk? How does she talk? How does she dress?

What does she do during her work hours? What are her goals and motivations? What are her challenges and how does she handle those? When she is confronted with someone who upsets her, how does she handle herself?

I must then practice acting the part to the degree possible at work and at home, so that it becomes a habit and a manner of thinking. I need to also begin to acquire the props that will bring this identity to life. If I think that the Headmistress would carry business cards, I need to work on creating and obtaining those. If I think she would wear a certain style of clothing, I need to make it a goal to acquire that clothing.

Adjusting to Life on the Outside

Joining a group of fellow former 9 to 5 prisoners who can identify with your pain and support you in the adjustment is important. They are the only ones who truly understand what you are going through. They can tell you what is normal and what isn't.

They can also remind you, when you start to look longingly back at the safety and stability of the prison, why life truly is better on the outside than it was on the inside. They can remind you of how cramped and confined you felt, what it was like to have every decision you made dictated to you, and of the reasons why you made your escape in the first place.

I am starting a Shine Academy Facebook page to help me start building a support group of former 9 to 5 prisoners, and I invite you to join it. The group will be free to join, and in it I plan to share daily tips on how to keep your mind-set right, your spirits up, and your purpose foremost in your mind.

Avoiding Recapture

To avoid recapture, you have to do the hard things. You must face up to your fears, put yourself out there, and risk rejection. You must use your gifts to serve others and risk being taken advantage of or being unappreciated by those you serve. You must grow your network and keep your ears and eyes open for opportunity.

You must also continue working when the business doesn't seem to be going anywhere, continue believing when there's no evidence of progress, and stay committed to keeping yourself out of confinement even when everyone around you is telling you it's time to give up and go back to captivity. The truth is your biggest danger isn't recapture. It's surrender.

> *"Life dishes to each of us what we need to grow, to overcome, or to triumph. It's up to us to first choose a path, and then a course of action as we travel down that path" - Clara Rufai*

Belief in yourself and a positive self-perception are non-negotiable in the journey to greatness. A broken spirit can only produce a broken life. Yes, storms of will hit, and like I always say 'pain' is universal, it will happen to everyone, old or young, big or small, high or low, male or female, black or white. But pain can, and should be viewed a something that teaches, instructs and strengthens you to be a better, stronger version of yourself.

As human beings, we don't necessarily expect or look forward to pain, but the truth is that the good, the bad and the ugly cards that life deals us - they all combine to make us who we are. Those who are more successful at processing and dealing with pain are those who have control over their mind. Acquiring emotional intelligence is a key component to living life successfully.

As I have travelled along my path in life, I have come to realise that equanimity is key, and this realisation has helped me cope during those times when life has dealt me some not-so-good cards.

I am now an advocate of the gospel of equanimity. I have learned how to assert to my unconscious mind the fact that I am 'master of my grouse' and I confirmed this to myself in a poem I wrote more than 15 years ago, entitled 'Kiss Of Dawn.'

This is what I see among those who have made their relocation to their Shine Zone. It's not an easy life, and not everyone is ready for it, but I am working toward the day when I can join them there. One of the women I've met who is living exuberantly in her Shine Zone is Coach Kemi Oyesola.

Meet Coach Kemi

Kemi always knew that she was not meant for 9-5 work. She worked as an Administrative Assistant in the Job Center and was headed toward the top but was sacked when her bosses heard her keep saying, "I'm supposed to be an Executive Officer this summer." She was ambitious, with big dreams and plans.

She went on to work in the London Regional Transport refund department where she was able to talk to people of all kinds and learn the rural network like the back of her hand. However, she hated the boring sameness of the journey to and from work each day. There was no adventure, no difference.

She also hated the feeling of needing to put on appearances for the sake of others. It felt like pretending rather than being.

Planning the Escape

Two weeks before the birth of her first -born daughter, Sarah, she resigned from that job. She miscarried a second time after her daughter's birth before giving birth to her son, Joshua, in 1994. While none of the pregnancies were planned, she thanked God for each of them.

She became a Consultant for Mary Kay Cosmetics and quickly moved up the ranks. She was headed toward the top when her marriage began struggling and, because she didn't have a firm grip on her emotions, the struggles spilled over into her business. She felt compelled to leave that line of work despite having built a team of 40 consultants.

Her next job was an answered prayer – a sales job across the street from her children's primary school. She was able to pick her children up after school and bring them to the office. Eventually, she reduced her work hours so that she could take the children straight home after school let out, choosing to take the salary reduction in order to prioritize the things that mattered most to her as a human being and a Mum.

She hated the limitations and the boring monotony of the 9 to 5 work. She also hated the gossip and the phoniness she felt was required of her. It wasn't in her to pretend that she was happy when she wasn't.

When she received a call to speak in front of a group of women in Kenya, she knew it was a call from God to serve His people. She offered to take time off in leave rather than resign, but her boss refused to give her the time off. His answer remained the same despite her presenting every reasonable alternative.

His refusal made it easy for her. She recognized it as a moment where she was being forced to choose between serving

God and serving the world. It wasn't in her to say "No" to God over a 9 to 5 job.

They were shocked when she resigned, but she knew it was the right decision for her. After returning from ministering to those women, she decided then and there that nothing would get in the way of her doing what she was meant to do or being who she was meant to be.

Whatever tried to stop her or stand in her way, even if it were her own children, would become dust before her. What others thought or felt did not matter, especially when she knew it was what she was called or born to do. She would grind or shift whatever stood in her way.

> *Having such a clear perspective of what I want, who I am, and where I'm going prevents a lot of unnecessary headache and time spent wondering whether I should or should not do things. This is me. These are my parameters and within these boundaries I am great. Anything outside of those is a no-no. I think you've got to know that and be bold enough to do it. – Coach Kemi*

Life After the Escape

She went through many trials after leaving the 9 to 5 work world. She became suicidal and filled with urges to kill her husband. Her hair was falling out in patches and she was forced to keep her head shaved to prevent people from seeing it. She was messed up and very angry, but she didn't see her behavior as abnormal at the time.

When she and her husband finally separated, she asked God why this was happening to her and to her marriage. She knew her marriage was not supposed to end. He told her it was because of her thinking.

She went and picked up a Bible, Bible commentaries, and every Bible resource she could find to see whether the word "think" was in the Bible.

For as a man thinks in his heart, so is he – Proverbs 23:7

That was the beginning of her How2Think program, but it would take her years before she would get into coaching. Three days after her husband left, she realized she was sick and needed emotional help. She tried counselling, but they were unable to provide her the help she needed.

She signed up with a coaching program and began studying classes at University. After graduating from the coaching program, though, she discovered she didn't know how to market her programs. She didn't know how to make money from what she'd learned. Despite her hard work, her many gifts, and her service to the church, success eluded her.

She tried everything everyone told her to do but nothing changed. She fell ill, and had to leave University for a year. She came back to graduate in 2012 and was evicted in 2013 because in spite of all her hard work, she still wasn't making any money. She didn't know how to market her program.

What seemed to be for the worst proved to be a great blessing in more ways than one. Within three hours they were re-housed in a halfway house that was much larger than the home they'd been living in. The eviction proved a breakthrough moment for her. She realized the reason her programs were not selling was because she didn't believe in them. Her thoughts were still in her way.

She travelled to Florida for a 4-day coaching seminar. The decision propelled her forward, as she continued to do the same thing she'd been doing but this time with belief in herself and the proper mind-set.

The more she taught her How2Think program, the better she became and teaching it helped her to overcome her own numerous fears. Her journey to break free was filled with many struggles, but she expresses no regrets.

She feels more fulfilled now than ever before and would do it all over again if given the choice because it is all part of making her who she is today.

Coach Kemi's Lessons on the Run:

1.   If it is to be, it's up to me. God is waiting for me to move and to deal with it.

2.   The church did not teach me well, but it is not their responsibility to do that. I have a responsibility to go and learn and correct whatever I've been taught wrong. No excuses. Nobody, not the church, not my husband, nobody but me has that responsibility.

3.   Faith is dead, completely dead without works. I've understood that now. As the body without the spirit is dead, faith is just as dead. The body isn't dead because your heart stops beating. It's dead because the spirit has departed. I can have faith, but if there is no work that goes alongside that faith, it is as dead as a body that is lifeless and cannot move. That faith will bear no fruit and nothing will come of it.

4.   I must be engaged daily and must work on me. I am meant to take notice of my faults. I must harness my thoughts rather than just allowing those thoughts to run through my mind. I must guard my mind.

5.   I must be very clear about who I have around me, what I have around me, who I watch, what I watch, what I listen to, and take no prisoners. My life is too precious.

6.   It is a thin line between death and life, and I was a part of the walking dead for a long time. I can't go down; I have got to take control. You are down before you realize you are down. That tilt

toward death can happen in a split second. Life is too precious. I have only ONE life, one opportunity to make a difference. I can't stand before God and blame others or blame my circumstances.

7. It's about being mentally and emotionally intelligent. The biggest battle is what goes on inside of you. It's not whether you have adversity and issues or trials and tribulations, because if your core is strong enough, you're able to understand everything and are able to find peace in any circumstance.

Moving Forward

Strategizing and planning are the advice that most people give, but for Coach Kemi, she prefers to plan as she goes.

Connect with Coach Kemi

Website: http://how2think.coachkemi.com

Twitter: @how2think

Facebook: https://www.facebook.com/How2Think/

AFTERWORD

Written with purpose and shared with love, Clara Rufai hopes this book will prove useful for those who want to discover and unlock their Shine Factor and relocate to their Shine Zone.

She is here to be your Enabler, Inspirer, and Cheerleader. Having walked the 9-to-5 lifestyle herself, she is interested in helping career women and entrepreneurs overcome the challenges of their busy lifestyles, break out of containment, and discover more sustainable alternatives for creating income, impact and influence.

Her greatest desire is to help women develop the mental toughness they need to help them escape the 'prisons' that hold them bound. Her special interest lies in working with career women who want to transition from the limitations of their corporate cubicle to living life on their own terms.

Clara believes that together we can build a powerful community of like-minded individuals, sharing our prison break stories, and helping each other connect with and shine in our personal brilliance.

She believes that community will eventually spawn a defiant movement of triumphant prison-breakers, people determined to say YES to their next chapters and to live out their best lives.

Ready to Break Out?

Get a FREE copy of Clara's Perspective Posturing Statements, Re-Posturing Exercises, and Reflection questions by visiting her Facebook page and signing up for her email list at https://www.facebook.com/clararufaiNBTC

If you would like a FREE Shine Factor assessment, you can contact Clara directly at clara@clararufai.com. She will be happy to schedule an appointment to speak with you in order to help you determine your Shine Factor so you can start working on moving into YOUR Shine Zone.

Also, sign up for Clara's email list in order to be notified when Clara's Shine Academy is up and ready. It will be jam packed with strategies to help people of all ages find and relocate to their Shine Zone. Learn more at http://shineacademyglobal.com

Readers Beloved, Reviewers Adored

Clara would love to know your honest opinions about this book and the content. Please consider leaving your review on Amazon.com. When reviewing, please consider answering the following questions:

1) What, specifically, did you like or dislike about it?
2) What was the most helpful piece of advice you found in this book?
3) If you found room for improvement, what would you like to see covered that was not?
4) What do you think should have been covered in more depth?

For More Information

If you would like to receive memes of some of the greatest quotes from the book, please email me at clara@clararufai.com.

If you would like to receive soft copies of the meme to use as wallpapers, screen covers, or just to share on social media, just ask.

Join me on my private Facebook page for more (discussions of the book, bonuses, giveaways and free coaching and advice on life lessons.

https://www.facebook.com/clararufaiNBTC